ALSO BY JAMES NOLL

The Topher Trilogy
Raleigh's Prep
Tracker's Travail
Topher's Ton

Short Stories
Thirteen Tales
The Wounded, The Sick, & The Dead

The Bonesaw Trilogy
The Rabbit, The Jaguar, & The Snake

The Hive (Serial)
Seasons 1-4

Stand Alones
Mungwort
Captain Commander & the space spiders… FROM SPACE!

Audio Books
Raleigh's Prep
Thirteen Tales
The Wounded, The Sick, & The Dead
The Hive: Seasons 1-4
The Rabbit, The Jaguar, & The Snake
Mungwort
Captain Commander & the space spiders… FROM SPACE!

BEING INDIE: TIPS, TRICKS, AND TACTICS FOR THE BEGINNING INDIE AUTHOR

Fiction * Audio Books * Film
www.silverhammer.studio

BEING INDIE: TIPS, TRICKS, AND TACTICS FOR THE BEGINNING INDIE AUTHOR. Copyright © 2019 by James Noll.

All rights reserved. Printed in the United States of America. No part of this book may be used or reproduced in any manner without written permission except in the case of brief quotations embodied in critical articles and reviews. PULP books may be purchased for educational, business, or sales promotional use. For information, visit www.jamesnoll.net

Book & Cover Design by James Noll

Author Photo by Haley Noll

ISBN-13: 978-1-7337443-3-1

For New Indie Authors Everywhere

CONTENTS

Introduction	1
Part I: Writers Write	7
Part II: The Author's Process	49
Part III: Marketing For Beginners	95
Final Thoughts	129

INTRODUCTION

I've been a drummer my entire life. For a long time after I graduated from high school (and while I was in college and a little while after that), the only thing I wanted to do was play music and make albums. I played in four bands, Clark's Ditch, BEEF JERKY, The Minus Men, and Alpha Jerk, and we toured up and down the East Coast, playing bars and basements. Sometimes we got lucky and scored an opening slot at a larger club, but mostly these were DIY, bootstrap organizations.

The albums we wrote, recorded, and produced were a natural offshoot of being in a (kind of) touring band. Although holding the final master of the first album I played on was pretty cool, producing our music wasn't just something we wanted to do. It was expected. If we showed up to a gig without merchandise (CDs, T-shirts, stickers, buttons), it made us look even less professional than we already were. It might be strange to say this, but the punk rock bands and fans we played with and for celebrated a very capitalistic, DIY ethos. They wanted to support us, and they did it by buying whatever we had to sell.

That's why, when I started my publishing odyssey in the late 1990s, I was shocked by the lack of respect DIY was afforded in the book industry. In music and film, anybody who produced their own album or movie was admired; in the publishing industry, it was called "vanity publishing." The difference in attitude struck me as strange and not just a little outdated.

And what a convoluted mess it was to get published! First, you had to find an agent willing to try to sell your work to a publisher. To do that, you had to research agents (in the pre-Internet days, this was done through guides like the Writer's Market), and once you found a handful of agents who think might be willing to read your work, send them a query (which amounts to a cold-call) and hope they might like your idea enough to make contact. Then there were the dozens of seemingly arbitrary submission guidelines. One agent might want a letter only, while another wants a letter plus the first chapter, while still another wants the whole manuscript as well as a prepaid envelope to send it back if they don't like it. Some threatened to ditch the whole thing altogether if the formatting was wrong. All this to end up in the slush pile and ignored anyway. Even if, after all of that, I got lucky and was picked up by an agent, there wasn't a guarantee that I would get published. If your agent couldn't sell the book to a publisher, it was back to step one.

On top of that, the gatekeepers never seemed to have any better handle on what was good and what wasn't anyway. Traditional publishing has given us amazing works of literature, and certainly there are bad indie books out there, but with over a million titles published a year, the trads have also produced plenty of books that had me thinking "Who thought this was a good idea?" This rings true for the other entertainment industries as well. I've listened to bad albums viewed terrible television shows and sat through boring and/or poorly made movies that were produced by major studious with huge amounts of money, talent, and creative pedigree at their disposal that were bad. It's interesting to me that, despite that fact, nobody has ever pointed to the latest Transformers movie, Black Eye Peas album, or Vampire Diaries spin-off as a reason to stop consuming major studio projects. In other words, I've never heard someone say "All major studio artists/directors are hacks" because a few bad artists made bad art. So to me, the idea that someone shouldn't try to write, publish, and market his or her book because "That's not the way it's done" or "There are examples of poorly written indie books out there" feels like something the gate-keepers say simply for the sake of keeping the gate shut.

And yet the old models remained stuck in the twentieth century with a pinky grip on the nineteenth. Unfortunately for the people who hung onto the old ways, we are well into the twenty-first century. Things have changed.

Staring in 2008, I started hearing grumblings about indie-publishing. Amazon was at the fore, sponsoring the Amazon Breakthrough Novel Award until 2014 when they launched their own publishing company. In the meantime, they'd already bought Createspace (now Kindle Direct Publishing), which, along with Smashwords, became an easy, affordable way to self-publish. Then Ingramspark came along, and Draft-2-Digital, and Kobo, and for indie-audiobooks, Findaway Voices. Coupled with self-published books being adapted into major motion pictures, such as The Martian and Fifty Shades of Grey, I think it's safe to say that the stigma of DIY publishing has been washed away. The Martian was selected as the winner of the 2014 Goodreads Choice Award for Science Fiction and the movie adaptation won the Golden Globe for Best Motion Picture.

The indie publishing revolution is in full swing.

Yes, many indie authors, myself included, are not able to quit their day jobs and go at it full-time, but that doesn't mean the opportunity isn't there. As I sit here writing this introduction, I'm pretty stunned by the developments of the four years since I used Createspace to publish my first book, A Knife in the Back. All of the modes of production have been streamlined, from editing and publication to marketing, accepting payments, and distribution. If you want to work at it, if you want to create content, run your own business, and even make a little money, technology has made all of the tools that you need affordable and available.

Who This Book Is For

This book is intended for anybody who is interested in, or who just started, writing, publishing, and marketing a book. Do you have a novel you've just been dying to complete but can't seem to get it done? Have you finished a book but don't know how to edit, publish, or market it? This book is for you.

PART I: WRITERS WRITE

Here's an illustration of tenacity. I wrote the first draft of what would become the bones of my first novel, *Raleigh's Prep*, over the course of fifteen years. I remember scribbling down scenes in a spiral notebook while sitting on a hill and simultaneously watching my oldest daughter (who was still in elementary school) play soccer. Then I scratched out draft after draft during breaks while working as a bartender, trying to ignore the reggae bands playing fifteen feet away. I worked and reworked that manuscript throughout my two years as an assistant librarian and my subsequent years as a High School English Teacher. Even after all of that, after all of the tweaking, perfecting, and editing, after I took the plunge and self-published it (as a part of *A Knife in the Back*), after I held readings and book signings, after I wrote two sequels (*Tracker's Travail* and *Topher's Ton*), I still couldn't see fit to refer to myself as a writer.

That's tenacity in two ways, one helpful, one harmful.

It wasn't until I started learning about marketing and selling my work to people who enjoy it that I finally became comfortable calling myself a writer.

Why?

Probably because of the old stigma. I still didn't feel official because an agent hadn't liked my book and a publisher paid me next to nothing for all of my labor. In other words, nobody had asked me to write the book, so I didn't count as a writer.

This is the first thing everybody interested in self-publishing needs to understand: once someone successfully writes, edits, and publishes a book, she is a writer. She earned it.

Writers write. Embrace the idea.

Creativity Is Difficult

On top of that, we are currently at the tail end of a cultural and educational focus on STEM, STEM defined as Science, Technology, Engineering, and Mathematics. I don't mean to disparage STEM at all. I'm writing this book on a MacBook Pro while listening to Pandora on my Sony noise-blocking headphones and enjoying Internet service compliments of the iPhone personal hotspot wirelessly connected to my computer's Bluetooth. However, the late addition of the Arts to STEM (making it now STEAM) seems like a typical oversight of the humanities.

Scientists, engineers, and mathematicians are educated and intelligent people. Many of them are fine writers. My point is to illustrate a fallacy that permeates our culture: that the arts are 'easy.' There are varying arguments that diminish the arts.

1. Anybody can write.
2. Art is entertainment, and entertainment is a want, not a need.

3. What entertains one person doesn't entertain another.

4. This subjectivity makes it easy to create something someone will enjoy.

5. There's no money in fiction.

While 2 and 3 are somewhat true, 4 and 5 are not. If 4 was true, then everybody who ever created something would be declared a genius. And if 5 was true, then why are Netflix, Hulu, Amazon Prime, CBS All Access, Disney +, HBO, YouTube TV, and myriad others so financially successful?

The total worldwide box office for the movie industry grew 1% in 2016 to $38.6 billion. [citation: http://www.latimes.com/business/hollywood/la-fi-ct-mpaa-box-office-20170322-story.html]. Netflix alone (a creative disrupter of the cable and network television and movie industries) earned $8.86 billion in 2016 [citation: https://www.statista.com/statistics/272545/annual-revenue-of-netflix/].

People can make a lot of money in the creative industry.

Update for 2023:

The 148 day writers strike just ended, and boy did they get a good deal. Better pay, better benefits, assurances that generative AI will not take over writers' rooms.

Creativity is not just a necessary component in just the arts anymore. After a decade of focusing on the importance of STEM, more and more non-arts-related businesses cite creativity as one of the top skills they're looking for in their employees, third only behind complex problem-solving and critical thinking (both of which, I'd argue, require creativity, but I understand the need to be specific.

[citation: https://www.ideatovalue.com/inno/nickskillicorn/2016/09/leaders-agree-creativity-will-3rd-important-work-skill-2020/ "Leaders Agree: Creativity Will Be The 3rd Most Important Work Skill in 2020"].

The reality is that creativity, the principal component in a successful career in the arts, is more difficult, more profitable, and more integral to business than people are willing to admit.

Because of this attitude, and because of the inherent isolation and self-doubt that is a part of the creative process, I designed this section to provide some tips, tricks, and tactics to help overcome the feelings of uncertainty (from both internal and external sources) that are bound to pop up at some point during the creative process.

So What's Stopping You?

One day in elementary school, my sixth-grade teacher, Mrs. MacDonald, gave the class an assignment to write a story. She didn't care what the story was about, just as long as we wrote one. I think I knew what I was going to write even before she finished explaining what we were supposed to do.

I'd spent two weeks with my grandparents the previous summer, and while they were at work, I was left to my own devices. Bored out of my mind, separated from my friends and video games and cable TV, I wandered around their house, poking through their cabinets and drawers and investigating their bookshelves. That's where I found a mystery novel. I don't remember the title, but I do remember it was set on a boat out at sea, and one by one, the characters started to get killed off. Also, the murder weapon was a knife that had been stuck in one of the planks. I know that's extremely vague, but the point is that the book captivated me. I was hooked. I called my grandmother every day and gave her an update on what I'd read, then we talked about it later when she got home from work.

That's why I decided to write a mystery story to complete Mrs. MacDonald's assignment. I named the characters after some of the kids in class, one of whom I described as a "three-time loser." I had no idea what that meant at the time, and I have no idea where I picked it up, but Mrs. MacDonald laughed when I read that part out loud to the class, and from that moment on, I knew that I loved writing, and I wanted to write my own stories.

Of course, the gauntlet that is middle school intervened, then high school, and I didn't try to write again until I was sixteen. This time, I was inspired by Harlan Ellison's "'Repent Harlequin,' said the Ticktockman." I first found that story in one of the many paperbacks that I think my brother bought, read, and left lying around the house. This one was called *World's Best Science Fiction, 1966*. After reading that story for the billionth time, I remember putting it down and thinking "I can write something like that." I'd been waiting for permission that I didn't need.

I went down to the family Commodore Amiga, a machine that had been used primarily for games of *Defender of the Throne*, and banged out my first short story in nearly four years.

It was terrible.

I remember giving it to my girlfriend at the time to give me some feeback. Her reaction after reading it?

"You should keep trying."

So I did.

I kept hacking away at storytelling throughout high school and college. I was never really happy with what I wrote, but that didn't stop me. I aimed for longer and longer pieces, things I intended to be novels, but which I could (for one reason or another) never complete.

In my early twenties, I got into H.P. Lovecraft, which was why, I suppose, the first novel-length manuscript I ever finished was a wildly unsuccessful weird tale set in Fredericksburg, VA. It was about massive worms and homegrown superheroes and some kind of Illuminati plotting the end of the world.

It was terrible, too.

At that point, though none of what I'd written amounted to very much in terms of, well, anything, it did give me something even more invaluable: practice, time, and experience. I estimate that by the time I was ready to self-publish my first collection, *A Knife in the Back* (2013), I'd put about nineteen years into writing. I'm pretty sure that surpasses Malcolm Gladwell's 10,000-hour mark, but I've always been a slow learner.

As of this writing, I've spent four years traveling to conventions, festivals, fairs, and other live events to market my books. I love meeting people at these things, and nearly all of them are interested in publishing and writing. I've spoken to professionals, retirees, professional retirees, high-schoolers, fellow vendors, teachers, convention volunteers, and a lot of them have said the same thing at some point in the conversation:

"I want to write a book."

My response is always the same.

"So what's stopping you?"

Eight years ago, when the gatekeeper system was still in place, when to get published someone had to jump through all of those hoops I discussed before, pointing to that system as an excuse not to write a book might have been understandable. Without the proper connections and prior publishing history, let alone publishing success, the chances of landing an agent let alone a publisher were astronomically low.

It still shouldn't have stopped anybody from actually writing, though. None of the bands I was in asked permission to write albums. None of the artists I know ask permission to paint, or draw, or illustrate. Writers shouldn't ask permission to write.

Here's what professional writers do: we write. We make writing a priority. We don't treat it like a hobby or a pastime. We sit down every day, in the morning before work, on lunch breaks, after dinner, in the fifteen minutes we have while waiting for the kids to get out of school, sitting on the sidelines during soccer practice, for ten minutes right before bed, and we get our words in.

Don't know where to start? Try writing 500 words a day for a month. The next month, try writing 1,000 words a day. At that rate, a writer can complete a draft of a novel in three months.

There is no magical point in some distant future when writing a book will become easier. There is no piece of paper that will validate the desire to become an author. There isn't a class you have to take, a book you have to read, or a process you have to complete before you're allowed to start.

If you want to be a writer, you have to write.

And write, and write, and write.

Failure Isn't Failing

I value failure almost as much as I value success. How do I know this? I spent over a decade developing two novels before I realized that the only thing worth salvaging were the protagonists. Once I let the failed novels go and let the characters I loved loose in a different setting, the three books that followed (*Raleigh's Prep, Tracker's Travail,* and *Topher's Ton*) flowed out of me like they'd been waiting there all along.

I'm not a glutton for punishment. I just really wanted those books to succeed. Plus, I knew the characters were good enough to have a better story built up around them, so I kept trying. And failing.

The first character's name is Topher, and he is arrogant, impetuous, and immoral, but extremely funny. I don't know where he came from, exactly, but when his voice first popped into my head, I remember thinking that I wanted to create a hero who, while a bit repellent, the reader couldn't help liking. Kind of like a less capable, less dashing, more buffoonish, but equally entertaining Han Solo. So, sure, he was an anti-hero, and that's what drew me to him, but he was my anti-hero, and he needed a plot.

The first novel he starred in was simply titled *Topher*. It was supposed to be comedic, kind of a blend of satire and farce in the tradition of *Catch-22* and *A Confederacy of Dunces*. The story went something like this: Topher stuffs the ballot boxes of a small beach town in Virginia to become the mayor. Once elected, he embezzles the town's money, buys a mail-order bride, and builds a subterranean casino with waterslides and cat races, hoping to turn the town into a tourist destination. Then a hurricane comes and wipes it all out, thus bankrupting the local government. To apologize, Topher holds a parade in his honor. The whole town shows up, hoping to tar and feather him, but upon their arrival, he releases a team of little people armed with water guns filled with cooking oil, dumps hundreds of pounds of confetti from the tops of the buildings, and is carried away into the air by a blimp shaped like a, well, shaped like something rather offensive.

So that novel didn't work.

But I liked Topher and his friends, Michael Zorn and Kenneth "Gertrude" Hughes, so much that I wrote a sequel in which they find themselves held captive in a different small Virginia town straight out of an episode of *The Twilight Zone*. I tried to write the plot so that the sense of the strange and unusual gradually unfolds: At first, everything seems to be going well. The men enter into something called The Gauntlet, which seems to be a series of games where international teams compete for some mysterious prize. Soon, however, Topher and his friends realize everybody who loses any of the games is killed. Though Topher and Co. end up winning the games, they are dismayed to learn that the prize is an eternity in Hell. That novel, *Igor's Inn*, was a little better, but it, too, failed.

But I didn't give up.

I'd always known that I wanted to write a novel about their past, an origin story, something having to do with the boarding school they attended as teenagers. However, I liked their personalities, their exaggerated egos, their buffoonery, their use of elevated diction, but I couldn't figure out how to write them as kids without losing all of those qualities. I struggled with it for a while before finally saying, "Screw it. They've always been that way." That's when I wrote *Raleigh's Prep*.

It was a mess from the start. Episodic, disjointed, and too zany, I had no idea what it was about or where it was going. But I just kept working on it: in the ten or fifteen minutes before work (I'd become a teacher by this point), while the girls were outside playing after school, in the few moments I had before bed. I dropped the project, frustrated with the lack of structure or momentum, but, refusing to let it go, I kept giving it another shot.

It took nearly ten years to punch, pull, and cut that story into something that resembled a novel. The *Raleigh's Prep* I published as a part of my first collection, *A Knife in the Back* (2013), was NOT the *Raleigh's Prep* I wrote by hand a decade before. Even after I published it, I continued to tinker with the text, cutting dialog tags, improving lines, until I got to the point where all I was doing was moving commas around and stopped.

The tenacity paid off. *A Knife in the Back* continues to be one of my better-selling titles at every event I attend, and it has garnered some nice reviews both on Amazon and Goodreads, including these:

"There are 7 short stories and a novella, plus the beginning of another story with some of the same characters from the novella. I enjoyed all the stories, but a couple of my favorites were 'Beta', regarding a remote village being terrorized by . . . something in the woods, and 'Under the Rocks', which dealt with a river and the monster therein. The novella was different as well; interesting characters, quite a lot of death and gore and some twists and turns"—Robin Abess.

"The standouts in this short story collection are Beta which is about a series of mysterious murders in a small village. It has an eerie tone reminiscent of old horror novels. 'City of Salt' is intriguing and left me wanting to know more about the post-apocalyptic world it's set in. Raleigh's Prep is witty and interesting."—Karen Reese

Even more importantly, the success of that novel led to the sequel, *Tracker's Travail* (which I included in *You Will Be Safe Here*), and which also received some nice reviews.

"[T]he author has done a good job of world-building here, the stories contain good characterization and solid action, and I greatly enjoyed them. Going into more detail would be doing a disservice to any readers who plan on checking these stories out.

Recommended, especially for fans of sci-fi fantasy or readers who simply appreciate a diverse and interesting collection of stories"—Dr. Gonzo

Thanks, Dr. Gonzo!

Encouraged by all of that, I finished the final book in the Topher Trilogy, *Topher's Ton*, in 2015, which I published in my third collection, *Burn All The Bodies*. As of this writing, I've published the first book in my new Bonesaw

Series, *The Rabbit, The Jaguar, & The Snake*, the entire *The Hive* series (four seasons with five episodes each), *The Encyclopædia Bizarre* (an illustrated book of hybrid monsters and their associated myths, lore, and stories, with art by Jamie Bronson), *The Wounded, The Sick, & The Dead* (a new collection of short stories), and I've planned the second book in the Bonesaw series, *Blood & Gold*.

Update for 2023:

Add another novel and novella to the list: Mungwort and Captain Commander and the space spiders... FROM SPACE!

So how did failure pay off for me? Look at it this way:

5: Number of years spent writing two failed novels (*Topher* and *Igor's Inn*)

150,000: Approximate word count of those drafts.

7: Number of years writing, rewriting, and tweaking *Raleigh's Prep*

2: Number of years "perfecting" *Raleigh's Prep*

12: Approximate number of drafts of *Raleigh's Prep*

54,000: Approximate word count of *Raleigh's Prep*

2: Number of sequels to *Raleigh's Prep* (*Tracker's Travail* and *Topher's Ton*).

16: Number of short stories I've published in addition to those novels

3: Number of books in my completed *Mad Tales* omnibus (*A Knife in the Back, You Will Be Safe Here,* and *Burn All The*

Bodies—which include the sixteen short stories and all three books in the Topher series.)

2: Number of new novels in my Bonesaw series: *The Rabbit, The Jaguar, & The Snake, Blood & Gold.*

4: Number of new novellas: Bonesaw vs. the Militarized Robotic Death Werewolf; Bonesaw's Baby; God's Bones; Captain Commander and the space spiders… FROM SPACE!

1: Number of new series: *The Hive.*

1: Number of new novels: Mungwort

9: Number of new short stories.

9: Number of audiobooks.

I spent a lot of years writing words that nobody will (thankfully) ever read, and while those were failed projects, I didn't let that get to me. I knew it was going to take a while before I perfected my process, so rather than giving up, I reframed each failure as steps along the way.

I know it's easy to repeat platitudes like "Never give up" and "You need to have grit," but it was only through not giving up and gritting my teeth through the failures that I got to the point where I am now. Honestly, though, it was always fun for me. I truly enjoyed it all.

So if you build a character or set of characters or a plot or a setting or a time period or a subject or a world that you love, find a way to write them. Don't worry if nothing works at first. Expect it. Have fun with it. Enjoy it. You will hit upon something. You just have to do the work.

Nonetheless, There Will Be Bad Days

Some believe that all it takes to write a book is a little imagination sprinkled with magic natural creativity and POOF! Book.

That is not true.

Most of the writers I know have been carefully learning the craft for years. They've put in their 10,000+ hours, written thousands of words, and edited thousands more. That writing a book requires creativity is a given, but people underestimate how much creativity it takes and how challenging it can be. On top of that, writing takes technical expertise, risk-taking, improvisation, critical thinking, and a host of other skills I don't even know about or forgot to mention.

That's not to say that writing is a chore. It's not. I love every aspect of it, from drafting through the final copy edit. I like the good days, when the dialog, description, and plot seem to flow out of me, and I feel unstoppable. I'd say that those days come more often than not.

However, there are also those days when the ideas don't come as easily, or when I spend an hour or two writing and writing but barely make it to four or five hundred words, or days where, sure, I've written a lot, but the dialog is stale, or the description cliché, or the plot meanders, and because I know more than half of it will be axed in the editing, my inner troll keeps telling me to drop the project altogether.

That's never really an option, of course. That's just my troll (I'll introduce him in a bit). Sure, some projects just don't work, but when you're just starting a book, never quit before you're done with the first draft. My students want to do this all of the time. Granted, they're young and just learning the craft, and yes, some merely don't want to do the work. The ones who are invested get frustrated if their first drafts don't immediately live up to their expectations. They'll come up to me when they're planning or plotting and say, "This isn't a good story."

Good Lord! How can anybody possibly know that before the writing is even started? Not one word is written outside a rough draft of a plan and already the project has failed?

So what happens when a project starts to fall apart? Try some of these tactics to get back on track.

Squash Your Troll

Everybody has a troll. A troll is that voice in your head that knocks you down, makes you feel stupid, and generally criticizes anything you try to do. Some people are excellent at ignoring their trolls. They know how to bat it away, how not to feed it. They can turn their trolls into little tiny ants.

But creatives are an entirely different bunch. The same qualities that make a creative, well, creative, also create some pretty nasty trolls. There is already a huge amount of self-doubt and insecurity rolled up in being creative because creativity by its very nature requires ingenuity and novelty, and being ingenious and novel takes a lot of hard work. There is also a certain amount of necessary failure in creativity, and that failure, while beneficial, can be difficult to take.

And here's the thing: Trolls are nourished by the insecurities with which artists naturally struggle, even when the work is going well, even when it's selling well. They feed off of negative energy, so when a creative is going through the much-needed critical thinking process, that person's troll, which might have been the size of an ant at one point, licks up those little drippings of fear and self-doubt and negativity and gets bigger and stronger until all of the sudden it's the size of a pit bull, an ape, or a grizzly. That's when it will be really difficult to ignore it, and all of the negative energy that is created by listening to it will just make the thing bigger.

My troll used to tell me a lot of things about my books and writing, my audiobooks, and my music projects: Your work is crap. Nobody's reading it. Aren't there more important things to do? This is stupid. You'll never make a living doing this.

"Why are even try? It isn't getting you anywhere."

"This isn't real work. Real work is toil. Real work pays minimum wage. You'll be lucky to even break even."

"This isn't making any money. This will NEVER make any money."

"Don't you think you should be [insert chore] rather than this?"

My troll didn't want me to make money or clean the house. It just wanted to increase my self-doubt.

If my troll were a person, I'd punch it in the face. I'd never listen to somebody who talked to me that way. Unfortunately, it's me telling me this, and while I wish punching myself in the face would get rid of it, my troll would just ridicule me for doing something that stupid in the first place.

Trolls love to sneak in at the most difficult part of the creative process. Here are a few tips and tricks that you can use to squash it and get on with the important stuff: writing and creating.

Write Something

Recently, I was listening to an episode of the *Self-Publishing Podcas*t (produced by the Sterling and Stone crew, Johnny, Sean, and Dave), and the guys were talking about their experience at a Robert McKee *Story Seminar*. McKee apparently said that creative writing is more difficult than brain surgery. That's an obvious exaggeration, but your troll doesn't care about that. All it cares about is the frustration and fear being creative can inspire.

For me, the difficult part of writing novels is the first draft. This was readily apparent when I wrote the rough version of *The Rabbit, The Jaguar, & The Snake*. Some days, the plot and dialog ran out of my fingers, and I could rock out a few thousand words in an hour. But there were just as many days that I spent three or four hours trying to come up with something, anything, and only managed about three hundred words of drivel. I hadn't lost my nerve or talent; I hadn't run out of ideas or gotten blocked. It was just really, really hard to write on those days.

And that's when my troll came knocking.

I've gotten pretty good at squashing my troll when I need to. One of the first strategies I learned from my friend Bill Harris. Bill is a successful artist who has created a career for himself as a painter. When Bill doesn't feel like painting, when his troll starts to whisper to him, here's what he does: he goes into his studio, picks up his brushes, and starts to paint.

Nothing frustrates a troll into silence than ignoring it and proving it wrong.

So the next time you've worked all day, driven the kids all over the place, cooked dinner, cleaned the house, remember that right then is when the troll is at its strongest. It will slime its way into your ear and say you're too tired, and what's the point of getting started so late? Why not just give up and have a drink and zone out in front of the television? Isn't there a new show on Netflix?

Instead of listening to it, pick up a pen or fire up the laptop, and DO SOMETHING. Even if it's only for thirty minutes, even if you make very little progress, even if you're not entirely satisfied with the writing, do it anyway.

Defeated, your troll will crawl back under its bridge.

Exercise

There is nothing better for creativity than exercise. In addition to releasing endorphins and improving your overall health, exercise unclogs creative blocks. It doesn't have to be anything super-exerting. It can be something as simple as taking a walk. I used unscheduled walks to help me develop the rough draft of *Bonesaw*. *Bonesaw* eventually became the bones (no pun intended) of *The Rabbit, The Jaguar, & The Snake*. I pantsed (more on that later) the whole first draft, so I came up with two self-imposed rules to get through it: each chapter had to follow a seven-step formula (more on that later, too), and no matter how gory or action-packed or science-fiction-y it became, I had to try to make it funny.

My overall strategy was to write for a few hours until I got to a point in the plot where I couldn't figure out what was going to happen next. That's when my troll found it easiest to act up. Sometimes it was loud ("you're NEVER going to finish this thing"), but most of the time it was a feeling of mild anxiety. Whenever it showed up, that's when I'd make sure to go for a walk.

First I'd jot down a few notes, usually in brackets, about where I thought the story might go. Then I put on my walking shoes and headed out into my neighborhood. My rule for the beginning of the walk was that I was not allowed to think about anything at all. I was only allowed to exercise. I pushed myself up hills, tried to walk faster until all I was focusing on was my heart rate and my legs. It usually took about ten minutes for my troll to retreat altogether (it hates cardio), and it was then that I told myself "okay, think."

This isn't a revolutionary strategy. There is plenty of research out there about the connection between exercise and creativity, and how taking time away from a creative project isn't just helpful, it's necessary. So if you're having a hard time with something creative, or your troll keeps getting in your way, go for a walk, go to the gym, lift weights, take a spinning class, do some sit-ups, do some yoga or pilates. Trolls prefer laziness and apathy. Exercise makes it run away and hide.

Take A Nap

The idea that more is better is a fallacy that continues to flourish, especially in America. In my experience, most of the people I've worked with who put in ridiculous hours and pushed themselves to work more and work harder were not very productive. They did tend to be inefficient or ineffective, and they certainly were not very creative.

Doing more might work with manual labor or tasks that don't require a lot of complexity, but it fails to be effective when it comes to creativity. When a creative pushes herself to do more, write more, create more, it just tires her out, and when a creative gets tired, that makes it easier for a troll to rear its ugly head.

So what improves creative productivity? Naps. However counterproductive it sounds, napping, particularly long naps (up to an hour or an hour and a half) is a major factor in boosting human creativity.

I'm not advocating for people to sleep all the time. That's depression. But a lot of indie-writers, myself included, already work day jobs. I'm a teacher. My hours are 7-3, and after making three presentations a day, grading papers, dealing with paperwork, and sitting in on meetings, I'm tired. I've tried to sit down and get my writing in right after I get home from school, but it doesn't work. I end up spacing out, staring, thinking about nothing, or wandering around the Internet. My troll loves this.

"That's right," it says. "Why even start? You're exhausted. Just do nothing."

But if I sleep for about an hour, I have all of the energy and focus I need to be creative. Napping makes me sharp, and my troll hates it when I'm sharp because I can very easily ignore it.

If You Want To Be A Writer, You Have To Read

I'm going to assume everyone reading this understands the connection between reading and writing. I'm also going to assume that the reason most of us became writers in the first place is because we love to read. I can still remember the moment reading suddenly made sense to me. I was about five years old, and I was sitting up in my room trying to read a Dr. Seuss book, and it all just clicked. I got so excited that I ran downstairs where my family was watching TV, a huge stack of Dr. Seuss books in my arms, and showed them what I could do.

I don't think I've looked back since. I remember falling in love with T*he Chronicles of Prydain, Dorp Dead*, and *The Lion, The Witch, and The Wardrobe* when I was in elementary school. My brother introduced me to Stephen King when I was in High School, and I ripped through everything he'd written up to that point, from *Night Shift* (which I read over and over) to *IT*. I still remember going to the bookstore at the mall to pick up a copy of *The Drawing of the Three* when it was released and sitting in my car to read the first two chapters. And, of course, I read *The Lord of the Rings* at least three times before my senior year.

I still read fiction every night. It's the only way I can get to sleep. I've devoured everything that David Mitchell has written; my favorites are *Cloud Atlas, Black Swan Green,* and *Slade House*. *The Book of Strange New Things* introduced me to Michel Faber. I didn't read *Under the Skin*, but the movie adaptation is excellent. When Donna Tartt released *The Goldfinch* to glowing reviews, I read that and her first book, *The Secret History*. *The Golem and the Jinni*, by Helene Wecker, was great, too, but my two favorite novels of the last decade were interesting takes on time travel. The first is *The First Fifteen Lives of Harry August*, by Claire North. The second is *Life After Life*, by Kate Atkinson.

I could go on and on about the books that I read, my favorites and my least favorites, but let me get to the main point: I write because I read. All of the books inform my imagination in one way or another. They influence me, either consciously or unconsciously.

And if you want to be a writer, you need to read, too.

Here are some suggestions for you to develop (or further develop) your reading habit.

Become An Expert In Your Genre and More

This is probably self-evident, but if you're going to write in a specific genre, it's important to become an expert in that genre. Most likely, you already like that kind of book (or that kind of television show or movie), so this shouldn't be a problem. However, science-fiction writers who have never read *Foundation, The Martian Chronicles, Dune, Brave New World, Ender's Game, Stranger in a Strange Land, Starship Troopers, Slaughter House Five*, or any of the other classic sci-fi novels or collections that I haven't mentioned, are going to have a hard time writing science fiction. Same thing for Romance, Horror, Action Adventure, or any other genre.

Becoming an expert in a genre provides the foundation a writer needs to be successful, the references, styles, tropes, moods, characters, settings, structures, and story beats. It tells writers which plots, themes, characters, and allusions have become cliche.

It isn't enough to read the classics. Since many genres overlap, look for the overlaps. Imagine a sci-fi writer who has read all of the books I mentioned and more. He loves *Star Wars* AND *Star Trek*. He's seen *THX 1138*. He's read those old sci-fi compilations (*The Best Science Fiction of the Year 1967*, etc . . .). He even keeps up with sci-fi being published today. He is an expert in his genre, and that's outstanding. But why stop there? Try crossing over into horror. The two are intrinsically linked. Read the classics: *The Other, Ghost Story, Carrion Comfort, The Turn of the Screw, Dracula, Frankenstein.* Soak up as much H.P. Lovecraft as possible. Read Poe. Read pot-boilers, hard-boiled detective fiction, anything that feels like it links up with your chosen genre.

This works for every other kind of book out there. Pick the one you love, become an expert in it, then find the logical crossover.

Vary Your Reading List

I thought I might start this section with some book reviews of some of the books I mentioned before (and some that I didn't). Don't worry, there's more of a point to this than just book reviews. So here is a list, in no particular order, of my favorite fiction novels of the last couple of years, along with a one-sentence description. There are some spoilers here, so if all you want are the book titles, don't read the descriptions.

The First Fifteen Lives of Harry August by Claire North—Like a more serious Phil from Groundhog Day, Harry August lives his life over and over again, retaining his memories and knowledge until he's over a thousand years old, at which point another one of his kind tries to destroy humanity, but he's too tired to do anything about it—just kidding; he tries to stop it.

The Book of Strange New Things: A Novel by Michel Faber– Peter Leigh, an ex-junkie turned Christian missionary, is selected to minister to the native inhabitants of the far-off planet Oasis (who have faces that resemble "a placenta with two fetuses—maybe 3-month-old twins, hairless and blind —nestled head to head, knee to knee"), while back on Earth the climate change ravages the world, and everybody turns to violence and tribalism to survive.

Your House Is On Fire, Your Children All Gone by Stefan Keisbye—One of the darkest and most disturbing books I've ever read, Your House is on Fire, Your Children All Gone has been described as a combination of The White Ribbon, The Village of the Damned, and every whacked-out episode of The Twilight Zone, the former of which involves horse mutilation, the blinding of an intellectually disabled boy, and nascent Nazism.

The Golem and the Jinni by Helene Wecker —One of my favorite parts is when the Jin gets the socialite pregnant—not the act itself, or the pregnancy specifically, but the weird changes the poor woman undergoes.

The Goldfinch: A Novel by Donna Tartt—Theo Decker survives a terrorist attack on the Metropolitan Museum, steals the titular painting, is shipped out west to live with his ne'er-do-well father, does drugs with his BFF, kidnaps his step-mother's dog, escapes back to NYC, is taken in by his mentor/father figure (who teaches him how to be an antique furniture dealer), and finally ends up in Amsterdam where he gets into a firefight with a gang of art thieves.

The Girl With All The Gifts by M.R. Carey—Every morning before school, the soldiers come into Melanie's cell and strap her to her wheelchair, making sure to fix her head in place just in case she tries to bite someone; that would be bad.

The Library At Mount Char by Scott Hopkins—The young adults in this horrifying fantasy novel (for adults) all have special powers given to them by "Father"—not their real father but a mythical figure who has . . . . adopted them: David kills everything, Margaret dies and resurrects herself, Michael talks to animals, and Carolyn learns every language ever written; when they are bad or disappoint Father, he puts them in a barbecue-shaped like a bronze bull and cooks them until there's nothing left but charred bones, then brings them back to life.

Borne by Jeff Vandermeer—Rachel, a survivor of an unnamed, worldwide ecological disaster, discovers the titular character (an amorphous jelly-like creature in the shape of an upside-down vase) stuck in the fur of a massive flying bear named Mord, fights the Mord proxies (vicious bears with venomous claws and are only able to say "Drrrk"), and resists the temptation of The Magician to join the fight against Mord; also, she has a boyfriend named Wick who has bio-engineered worms in his body that can help him heal: he may or may not be human.

Station Eleven by Emily St. John Mandel—Told from the perspective of characters who, in one way or another, have some connection to an aging movie star who has a heart attack on stage while performing King Lear (pre-apocalypse), Station Eleven is about a troupe of actors and musicians travel around a post-apocalyptic America after a super-flu wipes out most of the world, performing for the citizens of the little towns and hamlets that pop up in the aftermath, and trying to avoid any that might harbor cults and cult leaders, such as The Prophet, who is predictably A Very Bad Man Who Is Difficult To Defeat.

The Boy Who Drew Monsters by Keith Donohue—A little boy who almost drowns somehow gains the power to make his twisted drawings come to life; also, his best friend might be his half-brother because his best friend's mom seduced his father one drunken night after their parents had dinner.

Moonglow by Michael Chabon—Michael Chabon avoids using too much elevated diction and complex syntax to write the semi-biographical, er, semi-biography of his grandfather, who fought in World War II, really liked rockets, and hunted down a big snake that was eating the pets of the Florida retirement community where he lived after the death of his somewhat mentally-ill wife.

The Hapless Child by Edward Gorey—Children in Edward Gorey's classic tales do not fare well; nor do their dolls.

Honorable Mentions: Oryx and Crake, by Margaret Atwood, Slade House, by David Mitchell, and The Stolen Child, by Keith Donohue, The Reapers Are the Angels, by Alden Bell, and Lovecraft Country, by Matt Ruff.

Updated for 2023:

Fleishman is in Trouble by Taffy Brodesser-Akner—one of two the novels on my list that were turned into limited series. Fleishman is in Trouble follows the titular character whose wife cheats, leaves, and then one day drops off their kids and disappears.

Normal People by Sally Rooney—the second of two novels turned into a series. This book chronicles the love story between two young people who get together in high school, break up, get back together, break up again. It's a familiar story, but the two main characters are so well-written and likable that I found myself completely engrossed and rooting for them.

The Splendid and the Vile by Erik Larson—I'm a sucker for anything having to do with WWII, and apparently Eric Larrson is as well. Larson writes history like its fiction, which is probably why I'm drawn to his books. The Splendid and the Vile focuses on Winston Churchill and how he lead Great Britain through The Blitz. Spoiler alert: they drank a LOT of alcohol.

Runnin' With The Devil by Joe Laden and Noel Monk—For some reason, "Hot For Teacher" kept popping up on my Spotify feed a few years ago, and that led me into a deep dive back through their catalog. When their first manager published this tell-all at the tail end of my second obsession with Van Halen, I read it cover to cover in a couple of sittings. It's everything you'd expect from a tell-all about one of the hardest partying bands of the 80's. I don't think I'll ever forgive Roth and Van Halen brothers for the way they treated Michael Anthony.

The Dry by Jane Harper—this was the first book I read in a series of Australian murder mysteries. The plot revolves around Aaron Falk, who returns to the small town he left years ago after being blamed for the death of one of his best friends. He has to navigate the hatred most of the townspeople have for him while trying to solve a murder.

Cloud Cuckoo Land by Anthony Doerr—this book reminded me of another one of my favorites, Cloud Atlas. Multiple characters, multiple storylines, all of which intersect at some point. It's the only novel I've ever read that made me fall in love with a pair of cows.

FantasticLand by Mike Bockoven—after a hurricane strands a group of theme park workers at Fantastic Land!, they quickly turn on each other.

Tomorrow and Tomorrow and Tomorrow by Gabrielle Zevin—Sam and Sadie first meet as children and quickly bond over their love of video games. The novel follows them as they become successful video game makers and struggle with their relationships (with their boyfriends and girlfriends as well as each other). Zevin make video game creation sound exciting, mainly by focusing on it as a creative process rather than getting into the technical nitty-gritty.

I'm not a book snob. I'm not going to preach about the kinds of books every "good author" should read. If you want to read something, read it. However, sometimes a writer can get mired in the themes, characters, plots, and settings that are too typical of the kind of fiction she writes.

Two of the above, *The Girl With All The Gifts* and *The Reapers Are the Angels*, are post-apocalyptic zombie novels, my go-to plot of my go-to genre. The rest are Sci-fi or Horror, or a mixture of the two. The only odd man out on that list is *The Goldfinch*. It's imaginative, but I wouldn't call it Sci-Fi, Fantasy, or Horror. And I loved reading all of them, by the way, but by the time I finished *Lovecraft Country*, I felt as though I was on autopilot. The plots started becoming predictable, the characters a little run-of-the-mill. It wasn't the authors' fault; those books are excellent representations of their genre. I'd just read too many of them.

Consider the recent decade of blockbuster superhero movies. Now that CGI makes it possible to create anything a graphic novelist dreams up, and now that we've become used to seeing it, those movies are starting to be a bit of a chore. Why? Because barring a few outliers, they all seem to have the same plot: The Hero's Journey. Avatar is guilty of this. I love that movie. Amazing, groundbreaking effects. Awesome monsters. Action-packed battle scenes. But the plot is a combination of The Hero's Journey and The

Savior plot, in which the hero is transformed by natives he once tried to kill, becomes one of them, and fights on their side.

However, for every *Thor: The Dark World, The Amazing Spider-Man,* and *Superman Returns,* there's a *Legion* or a *Jessica Jones*. Both of the latter contain all of the familiar elements of the superhero plot. Tortured protagonist with special powers? Check. Call to Adventure? Check. Fall Into The Abyss Followed By Miraculous Return With More Strength? Check. But *Legion*, if you haven't seen it, adds layer after layer of David Lynchian weirdness to it, to the point where something that could have been a tired retread became new and exciting.

While *Jessica Jones* isn't as surreal, it does a great job standing the superhero story on its end, mainly through its snarky, alcoholic protagonist and the creation of Killgrave, one of the most disturbing villains in the genre. (He also has a pretty great name.) Killgrave, unlike the typical supervillain, doesn't want to take over the world. He just wants Jessica. Like, *want* wants her. Gross.

Both of them, however, use a profoundly literary approach: The Unreliable Narrator. The Unreliable Narrator is on full display in *The Catcher in the Rye, American Psycho, Lolita,* and any number of Poe short stories, from "The Black Cat" to "The Cask of Amontillado."

That's why it's important to vary your reading.

Don't worry about losing touch with your chosen genre; good storytelling is good storytelling, no matter what the genre. Adopting the different qualities of other fiction can benefit a writer in terms of introducing new, exciting, and creative voices, approaches, and structures.

Read Literary Fiction

One of the things I love about literary fiction is the way it plays with the typical narrative arc. That's not to say that literary writers don't use it. They do. It's just not a requirement, and if they do use it, it's not always so readily apparent. I like it when a novel doesn't follow an arc at all. Sometimes one will choose to engross me in beautiful imagery and amazing prose, like *The Poisonwood Bible* or *The Lover*. Sometimes they let me follow the non-scripted lives of amazing characters with interesting, non-linear lives, like *Middlesex* or *The Brief, Wondrous Life of Oscar Wao*. Literary fiction (what Stephen King calls *lit-tra-ture*) provides models of something other than just plot. It gives me a chance to ingest numerous styles, approaches, and purposes, and since being a creator requires the invention of that which is new, interesting, and entertaining, this is very important.

Read Biography

I loved reading Vonnegut in high school, but aside from *Slaughterhouse-Five*, his cameo in *Back to School*, and a vague understanding that he struggled with a misperception of his writing as "not literary enough," I didn't know much about the man. Reading his biography, *And So It Goes*, gave me a lot of insight into his depression and how much his experiences in WWII negatively affected the rest of his life and informed his work. I felt the same way about reading about William Tecumseh Sherman in *Fierce Patriot* and Ambrose Bierce in *Alone In Bad Company*. Reading *John Lennon: The Life*, *Steve Jobs* (by Walter Isaacson), and even Andy Summers' memoir, *One Train Later*, provides similar joys.

I don't use biography to rip off stories that happened to other people, but I do think a lot about the lives of the people I read about. How Vonnegut's sad-sack comedian routine was at odds with the way he treated his wife and sons. How Bierce's unrelenting strength of character and sense of humor gave him the wherewithal to survive numerous bullet wounds and, later on in life, stand up to a railroad titan. How Sherman overcame bouts of depression to become a celebrated war hero. How Lennon grew from a wife-beating, handicapped-mocking young rock star into a thoughtful father who worried that the concerts in Central Park would wake up his infant son while he was taking a nap. There are elements in the lives of these men to consider, depths of character to contemplate, transform, and inform your writing.

Flex Your Reading Muscles

I hated reading Shakespeare when I was in college and complained about it to anyone who would listen. It was too hard to read, too densely poetic. I felt like I was spending all of my time interpreting each line or listening to characters relay expository information. I also felt like I'd read all of the plots before, mostly because I had. I was just too thick-headed to understand that Shakespeare had popularized them four hundred years ago. I felt that way through a lot of the books and texts I read in school, and even though I waded through it, I did so begrudgingly.

I don't feel that way anymore. The value in reading challenging work goes beyond entertainment, and while I understand the idea of knowing one's audience, I also think that can be misinterpreted as "only give your audience what they're used to." My audience—any audience, for that matter—is smart. Readers enjoy books that offer a challenge and a surprise, and authors will go a long way to providing that by challenging themselves in their reading.

(One quick aside: That's not to say I believe in making a book difficult for difficulty's sake. I'm just saying that readers like a challenge and are frequently, if not always, bored by convention.)

So how does a writer challenge herself? I don't think you should go out and start trying to interpret graduate-level physics textbooks or start muddling through *The Faerie Queene*. Maybe start with something that uses elevated diction or complex syntax. Try something that presents archaic ideas or concepts. On one level, reading like this can help improve vocabulary and sentence structure, and it can present new ideas or new approaches to old ideas to store away for later use. It's amazing how these kinds of things can, either purposefully or subconsciously, seep into one's writing.

For a true challenge, read Shakespeare. It isn't necessary to read every last thing he wrote. Pick a popular play or two. Join a reading group to discuss it or find a way to teach some of it. For me, teaching *Macbeth* was a revelation. I had to know it back and forth to be able to sell it to classes of disinterested high school seniors, so I took my time reading it. I broke down each scene, interpreted my favorite lines. Here's one from Act I, Scene 2, as the Sergeant is explaining Macbeth's triumph on the battlefield to King Duncan:

"For brave Macbeth--well he deserves that name--/Disdaining fortune, with his brandish'd steel,/Which smoked with bloody execution,/Like valour's minion carved out his passage/Till he faced the slave;/Which ne'er shook hands, nor bade farewell to him/Till he unseam'd him from the nave to the chaps,/And fix'd his head upon our battlements."

Macbeth cut a guy in half from his stomach to his jaw, then decapitated him and stuck his head on the castle wall. Poetically. Shakespeare wrote heavy metal lyrics four hundred and seventy years before Dio.

Shakespeare isn't a pleasure read. At least at first. Don't read them in bed or at the beach. You won't get very far. Instead, treat his work like an assignment. To stay engaged, underline meaningful passages as you read. Stop and make notes in the margins. STUDY the work, don't just consume it.

Part I Top Five Takeaways

1. Writing requires that you put one word after the other until you're done. Write every day until the project is finished.

2. Great writers write bad stories, too. Failing is all a part of the creative process.

3. Squash your troll.

4. Become an expert in the genre you want to write, but . . .

5. don't isolate your reading habits. Branch out.

PART II: THE AUTHOR'S PROCESS

Fiction writers tend to break down into two different kinds: Planners and Pantsers. The definitions are pretty self-evident. Planners plan out their novels and stories down to the last detail and follow the plan. Pantsers start writing and see what happens.

I'm more a plantster. I believe in coming up with some kind of plan, but I don't mind following a plotline that digresses from it if the ideas end up being more interesting than the outline I made. In other words, if something cool pops up during the writing, I follow it and adjust accordingly.

I wasn't always this way. When I started writing almost thirty years ago, I was a proud pantser. I was a pantser up until I started teaching creative writing. For anybody who has never taught, walking into a classroom filled with twenty to thirty teenagers and saying "write what you want" is hardly a curriculum. Some people do understand story structure without being able to label the parts, but the only time I see that is when they are rabid readers. Most beginner writers need examples, structures, and strategies to make it work. If they don't have something to follow, they might be able to start strong but will (most of the time) get lost in the middle, digress, or glaze over their climax and drone on and on and on.

So I learned how to employ a narrative arc. I learned how to create conflict, elevate obstacles, and delay the reader's gratification. Since I knew I was going to have to help my students when they got stuck, I wrote along with them, hit my walls, and figured out how to get over them. Once I started using the, admittedly, tried and true methods of storytelling, my fiction began to improve. That is the value of planning.

The purpose of this section isn't to advocate for one and only one structure. It is to provide a few structures and strategies that can come in handy, from brainstorming to the final draft.

Brainstorming

A long time ago, I started to learn how to play guitar so I could contribute songs to one of the bands I was playing in at the time. After figuring out a few basic open chords, I found that songwriting was a lot easier than I thought it would be.

"Sure," one of my guitarist friends said. "At first."

The same thing applies to writing fiction. Once I figured out a few strategies that I could use to write short stories, I set out to write my version of the different horror fiction tropes. I wrote a vampire story (I call it my "not-vampire" story), a haunted house story, a ghost story, a zombie story, a werewolf story, a couple of serial killer stories, a post-apocalyptic monster story, a Rappahannock River monster story. (I admit that "Rappahannock River Monster" isn't a trope, but think of it as Fredericksburg's version of *Stand By Me* meets *The Creature From The Black Lagoon*.)

I was able to get thirteen short stories and three novels out of my initial burst of creative energy, but after that, I kind of hit a wall. In other words, it was easy. At first. Because I didn't want to repeat myself, I had to come up with some brainstorming strategies. To do that, I used a device I stumbled across on the web. It's called the Morphological Matrix, and though it sounds clinical and way too important for what it is, it's a handy tool for generating new, surprising ideas. Here's how it works:

Step 1: Create a chart with four column headings: Character, Quirk, Goal, Obstacle. Make as many rows as you like, but somewhere between five to ten seems to suffice.

Step 2: Fill in the blanks. Try to do it without any preconceptions of how they'll fit together in the end. (In other words, fill in the blanks at random.)

Step 3: Make five random connections between each heading and five "on purpose" connections.

Step 4: Write down your combinations like this: Character with a Quirk must Goal despite Obstacle.

Step 5: Pick your favorite combinations.

On the next page, I recreated the matrix that I used to jumpstart a new short story collection a few years ago.

A Character	Quirk	Goal	Obstacle
An old man	AIDS	research the invasion	inferior weapons
A teenaged girl	racist	kill a vampire	dehydration
A Texas Bureaucrat	uncontrollable physical ticks	steal a sacred amulet	lack of supplies
An Invading Alien	a head cold	defend home	the collapse of civilization
A Vampire Hunter	a broken leg	travel back in time to stop a nuclear accident	a hurricane
A Breast Cancer Survivor	memory loss	destroy the hive	a political coup
A Depressed Detective	overinflated ego	survive a witch	terrorists taking down the electrical grid
A Private in the Confederate Army	violent outbursts of anger	escape a kidnapping	tribalism
A Washed up Rock Singer	no empathy (superficial)	outsmart a pursuer	a murderous nobleman

Here are the combinations I wrote down:

1. A racist vampire hunter must survive a witch despite terrorists taking down the electrical grid
2. A private in the Confederate army with an overinflated ego must defend his home despite the lack of civilization.
3. A washed-up rock star with inoperable brain tumors must kill a vampire despite a hurricane
4. A depressed detective with a broken leg must destroy the hive despite inferior weapons.
5. A teenage girl with violent outbursts of anger must destroy an evil village despite dehydration.

It's interesting to note that I didn't end up using these specific combinations. After a few false starts with number five, I realized I wanted to mix and match the best elements of all of them. Here's the one I finally settled on:

6. A teenage girl with a broken leg must destroy the hive despite inferior weapons.

That story turned out so well that I decided to base four more on the main characters, Amanda and Bill Jett from Spotsylvania County, VA, who are caught in the middle of an alien invasion. And that's how I ended up writing *The Hive*.

The Narrative Arc and The Seven-Step Story

Every story has an arc. Some are more experimental than others, some more complex, and some stick exactly to a formula. I think of the arc in the same way I think of pop music. Pop music has one basic structure that musicians play around with. It goes like this: verse, chorus, verse, chorus [bridge/middle eight]; verse, chorus, end. The Beatles established themselves by using this structure. Listen to early songs such as "I Wanna Hold Your Hand," "Can't Buy Me Love," and "We Can Work It Out" and you'll hear it.

Sometimes the song will repeat the bridge ("We Can Work It Out") or come out of the bridge and into some kind of solo; sometimes the song will forgo a solo and repeat the chorus twice (or fade out repeating the chorus.) Whatever the case, there is a structure, and people love listening to it. A lot of the enjoyment of music comes from the old paradigm of building suspense and anticipation. The listener, knowing that a catchy chorus is about to come up, gets more excited, and then when it hits, they sing along. They LOVE that song. Jokes operate on this model, too. They follow a formula, lead the audience down a specific path, use some misdirection or irony, and then deliver the punchline. We're familiar with these structures and use them to determine whether or not we like a song or a comedian.

Narration, at its most basic form, is like this, too. Good stories (stories that we love) tend to follow an arc or a variation of the arc. (Again, NOT ALL OF THEM. Some stories are awesome regardless of structure. I'm talking about stories that are mass-consumed.) Reading those stories can be like listening to a song that meanders or doesn't create suspense and anticipation or listening to someone who doesn't know how to tell a joke—they remain in interminable exposition, or they forget a detail that will make the punchline work, or backtrack, or they mess up the punchline.

Most people are familiar with the narrative arc. If you're not, here's a simplified version:

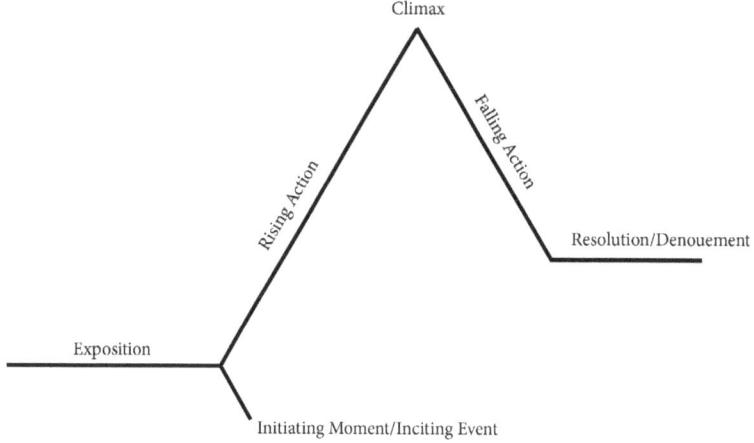

The definitions are fairly simple, too:

Exposition: Background information, setting, characterization.

Initiating Event/Inciting Incident: the moment that thrusts the reader into the main action of the story.

Rising Action: the events that create suspense and tension.

Climax: the release of suspense and tension.

Falling Action: the moments immediately following the climax.

Resolution/Denouement: the strands of the plot are drawn together, and everything is explained or resolved.

The pantser in me hated using the narrative arc, at least until I pantsed my way into several unreadable manuscripts. But there is an energy and sense of joy that comes out of pantsing a plot. I will say this: it wasn't until I planned my stories using the arc that my fiction started to improve.

Stick to the arc, don't stick to the arc. Plan it out entirely or sketch an idea and use it to head in the right direction. It's a good tool.

The Seven-Step Story

As useful as the arc is, the seven-step story is even more useful. I first came across it when I wanted to teach my students how to write longer work. Many of them felt that legitimate fiction was long. I didn't want to say "write more" or "introduce more conflict." Vague instructions never helped anybody develop anything. I happened upon a solution when reading the appropriately monikered Edo Von Belkum's *Writing Horror*. Von Belkum defines the seven-step structure as:

1. A character.

2. In a context.

3. With a problem.

4. An attempt to solve the problem.

5. Unexpected Failure.

6. Another attempt to solve the problem/Success or Failure.

7. Validation.

Other sources define the seven-step structure as variations of this:

1. Hook

2. First Plot Point

3. Pinch 1

4. Mid-point

5. Pinch 2

6. Second Plot Point

7. Resolution

Either one of them will suffice. Not only does this kind of structure fit nicely into the narrative arc, but it both lengthens the plot and introduces obstacles for the main character to overcome. Keeping your protagonist from achieving his or her goal develops suspense and creates tension, and suspense and tension (in any genre, from horror to romance) is what makes a story interesting.

Here's how I used the matrix combined with the Seven Steps to plot out the first story in *The Hive and Other Stories*, "Best Dog I Ever Had":

Matrix: A teenage girl with a head cold must save her father from the pod people despite being outnumbered by pod people.

7-Step Story:

Characters: Daddy & 'Manda

In a context: head into town for a field hockey tournament tour

With a problem: they wake up the next morning and their bus has been nearly destroyed (tires slashed, windows busted, engine block melted).

1st Attempt: Daddy's pissed but there's a mechanic right there (of course) who offers to fix it just around the corner.

Unexpected Failure: 'Manda waits and waits, but Daddy never turns up. She goes to the mechanic but nothing's there. She's attacked and has to escape. Rescued by her nemesis: Shelly Mae.

2nd Attempt: They track Daddy down

Success: Saves him.

After several false starts, I realized that the narrative wasn't working. How did I know? I couldn't move past the Exposition. I needed characters to interact, and when Daddy disappears, it just wasn't working. So I reworked the matrix idea and used the Seven Steps to revise the plan. I ended up with this:

A character: Clive Jett, a detective from Spotsylvania County, VA. He's thirty-four, recently divorced, and suffering from a recent (and very embarrassing) breakdown. The breakdown is the result of a mound of stress that occurred when he made national headlines for shooting a man he thought was a suspect in a convenience store robbery but who ended up being innocent. Also, he's broken his leg playing basketball, something his therapist recommended to help alleviate the depression.

In a context: A large, hive-like thing has been discovered out in the country by one of his friends, who calls in a panic.

With a problem: People have been going into the hive and not coming back out. Until recently.

First attempt to solve: he and his buddy agonize over what to do, but they settle on trying to shoot it. They do.

Failure: and the thing absorbs the bullets, shuddering. Icky green goo splatters out of the hive, hissing on the ground. Then a woman slides out of an orifice in the front. It's one of the victims. She speaks for the hive. Tells them to leave "us" alone. Then she melts.

They're facing a moral problem: do they blow the thing up or try to save the victims?

Second attempt to solve: They decide to tie a rope around one of the braver men and let him go in and detonate an explosive to kill the thing off.

Failure? Success? The thing glurps out some of the victims to try and stop him, but he kills them. At the last second, it vomits out a stream of the goo and, though he begins to melt, he manages to toss the bomb in the hive.

Validation?: Gray area ending? Clive gets his badge back. Maybe saves a few people. But maybe he begins to see evidence of its return (green glowing eyes? some kind of clue)

Rather than plot everything out using the Seven Steps again, I got started writing. What can I say: I'm a plantser. I used the characters from my original idea (Amanda and her father) and modified the steps to make them fit the new narrative. This time, and with further tweaking and pantsing (Amanda ends up being the one with the broken leg), the story worked, and I was able to complete the entire series for *The Hive*. If I were to set up a narrative arc for the first story, it would look like this:

The Narrative Arc

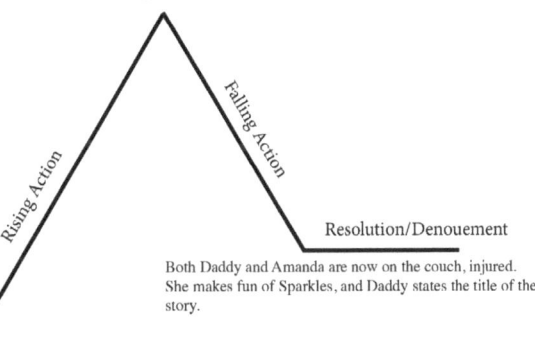

One of the tentacles catches the truck. Amanda is almost killed but manages to escape. The hive eats the truck and Daddy sets off the explosives.

Climax

Daddy and Amanda drive out to the Gomez's farm. Several neighbors are there, all armed. Mrs. Gomez freaks out and runs for the hive, her sons try to hold her back. Tentacles grab them. Daddy and the neighbors fire at the hive but it grabs them, too, ad everyone but Amanda is caught by the tentacles. She gets in the truck to send it, and the stuffed-dog filled with explosives, into the hive.

Rising Action

Falling Action

Resolution/Denouement

Both Daddy and Amanda are now on the couch, injured. She makes fun of Sparkles, and Daddy states the title of the story.

Exposition

Amanda explains how she wound up with a broken leg. She talks about her father and their farm. Then they feel what seems to be an earthquake.

Initiating Moment/Inciting Event
Gomer Gomez, one of their neighbors, calls to say a huge hive has landed on his barn. He's angry. He's going to shot it with his rifle.

Sometimes the matrix, the arc, and the seven steps work like this for me. Other times, the story pops out fully formed in the plans, and I don't have to work so hard to get there. The important thing to remember is that a process for planning that works for me, one that anybody can use to generate ideas and plots in any genre.

The Drafting Process

Every writer has his or her way of developing a short story or a novel, but when it comes down to it, there are three stages: Development Drafting, Line Editing, and Copy Editing. Development Drafting breaks down into two parts with multiple drafts in between. Part I: Rough Drafting. Part II: Beta Drafting.

My rough drafts can take up to five different passes, with a week or two between passes. All I'm trying to do is develop the plot, subplot, and characters. How many passes I make depends on what I'm trying to achieve. If I'm following a standard arc, the number of passes might be less. If I'm doing something non-linear (like I did with *The Rabbit, The Jaguar, & The Snake*), it might take more.

A Note On Professional Editing

If you're able to afford a professional editor, hire one. They can be expensive. Some charge by the word. Some charge by the project. They offer a variety of services, too. A comprehensive edit (development, line, and copy editing) will cost more than, say, a single copy edit. Make sure to shop around and look for the right fit. Don't expect someone who edits Romance to be able to edit Science Fiction (unless the editor specifically tells you she does both). Follow your gut, too. Sometimes personality clashes happen. Ask for a sample of what they can do. Pay them to edit a page or two of your work so you can see what they can do. Finally, beware of predators. There are a lot of unscrupulous people out there, so make sure to get a contract that details exactly what they're going to do, how much they will get paid and when, as well as a timeline for deliverables.

That said, there is nothing more valuable than receiving quality feedback from a good (human) editor. Beta Readers are wonderful sounding boards, but the right professional editor will help develop your work to be the best it can be.

The Development Drafts (aka The Madman)

Here's the rule I follow for all of my rough drafts: Finish the work.

That's it. Finish it so I can move on to the other stages. I know that the draft isn't going to be that great in a variety of ways, but I ignore that niggling insecurity to produce, produce, produce.

Here's a more detailed explanation of what that looks like.

Employ your inner Madman. The Madman (the part of your writing personality that completes the Rough Draft) is exactly what it sounds like. In creative writing, the only purpose of a rough draft is to give the writer a general idea of the direction towards which she wants to move. In The Madman stage of writing, allow yourself to be, just like the name implies, as crazy and as inventive as possible. Take risks, be weird, make things happen because it needs to happen (a cardinal sin in the final draft, by the way).

Speeling errars down't mater. punctuation errors, don't matter. The Madman gives you, as the creator of the rough draft, permission to have fun, see what happens, and be happily surprised at some of the outcomes.

I think of every draft that I put my work through during the Madman stage as a Development Draft. The first one is outright bonkers (as it should be), and while every draft after that requires a Madman mindset, they get progressively less insane. I find plot holes and fill in the gaps. I find inconsistencies in characterization or dialog and fix them. I foreshadow twists or add information that is important to understand the ending. Generally, my characters and plot follow the rules of whatever world I've built more closely, and the plot is pummeled into shape.

When I first started writing, I gave a few novels as many as thirteen or fourteen developmental drafts. Now I can generally narrow that down to five to eight (depending on the complexity of the plot, characters, and style). I also make sure to take time off between drafts. My general rule is two weeks to a month between novel drafts and a week or two off between short story drafts. To keep my chops sharp, I usually work on something in between drafts: a novel, novella, or short story, or, since I produce my own audiobooks, I'll narrate, edit, and mix and master those. That way I can shift back and forth between projects and keep my production engine humming.

The Editor

Once you've whipped the ideas, plot, and structure of your book into as good as shape as possible, and when it isn't possible to develop it any further, it's time to lock The Madman away and let The Editor into the room.

The Madman has long, unruly hair and forgets to shave. The Editor is a little more polished. Sure she wears frumpy cardigans and has ink stains on her skin and pencil dents in her fingers, but she's a pro. The Editor is the one who fixes all of the stuff that you (somewhat) neglected when The Madman was going crazy with the plot and characters and everything else. I let The Editor have at least two passes at everything I write. That's two passes of line edits and two passes of copy edits.

Line Editing

The purpose of a line edit is to make sure the syntax (sentence structure) and diction (word choice) are appropriate for the text. Is this word too scientific? Is that word too informal? Oh my god, I use [insert word] way too much. How many times have I used this similar syntactical approach? How many times have I started a paragraph with a particular strategy? Why did I think this simile was appropriate here, and why am I hammering the reader with that extended metaphor?

Here's a trick to making your line edits count: after a first pass, read your work aloud. You'll be surprised how many poorly worded sentences, clunky dialog, and other artistic missteps you catch. Be careful, though, of letting your troll in too much during this stage, and be careful of letting a read-aloud dictate too much of your line edit. Once the editing gets to the point of switching out synonyms over and over, it's probably time to move on.

Copy Editing

The purpose of a copy edit is to do all of the things The Madman throws to the curb. All of the grammatical, spelling, and other mechanical errors need to be fixed. It's the most technical part of the editing stage. I save this for last because it's more important to get the story told (The Madman) and told well (The Line Editor) before I start worrying about punctuation. After the first pass, I use Grammarly.com. Grammarly isn't perfect by any means, but it does help catch a lot of mistakes. For example, I'm terrible at placing hyphens in the right place during my development and line editing. Grammarly helps me with that. I also tend to add double articles (the the) and conjunctions (and and). Grammarly catches them.

It's important to take some of the suggestions the application makes with an eye for the art you've created. In other words, don't just blindly click through and accept every change it suggests. Just because it wants to put a comma somewhere doesn't mean it's right. Also, you have to have a pretty strong handle on grammar to use it. If you don't know the difference between an independent and dependent clause or how to use a semi-colon, using Grammarly might cause more problems.

After a Grammarly edit, I give my work one more pass before sending it off to my Beta Readers. Just like with a line edit, if you get to the point where you're just moving commas around, stop.

The Judge

If the Madman runs around in his underwear, and the Editor wears (un-ironed) pants, then the Judge comes to work in a three-piece suit. The Judge is the one who decides whether or not your work is worth publishing. Once again, do note that you should NEVER let the Judge in until you're sure you've done the best job you can, and definitely don't let him in if you're not done with the project. Some of my students want to talk to him while they're still brainstorming ideas.

Don't.

Letting the Judge in at any point in the drafting stage, all he'll say is your work is terrible, that someone has already done it better, or that the idea is too hard to complete, or that your sentences are no good, etc . . . . Most people who ditch projects before they're complete listen to their Judges way too early in the process. Listening to him before there's enough material to warrant his invitation will kill the motivation to write.

Since my first instinct upon finishing my development drafts is to say "Of COURSE the book is publishable! I wrote it, didn't I?" I make sure to get feedback from my Beta Readers before calling my Judge.

What's a Beta reader? A Beta reader is a product-tester. This is someone who reads your book in its "almost but not quite ready to publish stage" and gives valuable constructive feedback. I used my mailing list and a Goodreads thread to ask for one to read my novel *The Rabbit, The Jaguar, & The Snake*. Of the four people who responded, one read the whole novel and gave me amazing feedback (thank you Duane Pye!). I've also gotten Beta Readers through Goodreads giveaways. I sent off thirty copies of my first book, *A Knife in the Back*, and received feedback from fourteen of them. This cost some money

($4.10 for each book plus $6.75 for postage), but the reviews were very helpful. I've also run free deals for my second book, *You Will Be Safe Here*, and got a review/feedback out of that, too. Finally, it is possible to hire professional Beta Readers.

Good Beta Readers are priceless. They help fix little things like continuity errors, misspelling a name, problems with the timeline, historical mistakes, believability issues, and atmospheric missteps. They can also help in larger ways. Duane's feedback on the capricious nature of the early drafts of *The Rabbit, The Jaguar, & The Snake* helped me create higher stakes and give the entire novel a sense of purpose. With the other books I've published, when I received excellent feedback from my readers, I made some changes and re-uploaded the book. (That's the beauty of the self-publishing, POD model, by the way).

I will finally let the Judge in after all of that. My Judge tells me what works and what doesn't. He tells me which notes from my Beta Readers to take and which to ignore. He catches ideas that I've used before or that are too close to another work. He tells me whether I should shelve the project or take some time away from it before I give it another edit. Once he's done, I kick him out of the room. If I let him stay too long, he turns into a mean, little troll, and trolls are creativity killers.

The Importance of Word Counts

Whether you like it or not, specific kinds of fiction require a range of word counts. Here are some numbers to consider:

Kind of Fiction	Word Count
Flash Fiction	100-1,500
Short Story	2,000-7,500
Novelette	7,500-17,500
Novella	17,500-45,000
Novel	45,000 and up
Epic	Over 110,000

There are even more specific word counts for novels in specific genres. There are no hard and fast rules, but horror, mystery, and thrillers tend to be between 70,000 and 90,000 words, while Fantasy novels can be between 90,000 to 120,000 words. Romance novels can be between 50,000 and 100,000, and YA might be somewhere between 50,000 and 80,000.

Understanding word count is important for two reasons:

Audience expectations and productivity.

Audience Expectations

Your audience has expectations not just of the story beats, tone, and characters, but length. Writing a 50,000-

word Fantasy novel will disappoint your audience. Unless you're Stephen King, a 120,000 horror novel might be too much.

Productivity

It helps to know how many words you need to write every day during the rough draft stage. Since I write horror fiction, I'm aiming for an 80,000 to 90,000-word manuscript. While I'm working on multiple projects (and working full-time), I can get an average of 1,500 words in a day, so I can count on a draft being done in about two months. Some people write as many as 10,000 words a day. Some people write as few as 500. It doesn't matter how many you write, just as long as you write. Hitting a word count provides a window into how long it will take to complete a draft.

Fix it in the mix

Terry Pratchett once said that "a first draft is just you telling yourself the story." In other words, writers have to have something to work with before worrying about how good it is. It's going to be messy and imperfect, which is why throughout those early drafts I repeat the phrase "fix it in the mix" when I come across a problematic plot point or character or anything that gets in the way of finishing the work.

"Fix it in the mix" is something we use in the studio all the time. If a recording engineer can't get a specific sound he wants, or a musician is having a rough day nailing a guitar line or a drum part, sometimes, to save time and money, the band will fall back on this strategy. It means editing several takes of a guitar solo together to create one seamless one or using some studio tricks (reverb, side-chain compression) to achieve the sound they want. The key is not to use it as a crutch but as a way of getting the project done.

This can work for writing, too. When it comes to books, "fixing it in the mix" means not worrying about nit-picky details too early in a draft, knowing that it can be improved later on. It's more important to get something to work with first and fine-tune it later. Anything else feels like perfectionism, and if there's anything I want you to take away from this section it's DON'T BE A PERFECTIONIST. It will stifle your creativity and make it possible to complete your work.

But what about grammar? Spelling? Plot holes? How will my story be any good if I don't worry about them? Aren't they important? Of course, they are, just not in the beginning. What's more important is finishing the story in a very rough fashion. Worry about that stuff later during the fine-tuning of the Line and Copy Editing stages.

What are you allowed to do? Anything. Do you suddenly need your protagonist to use a weapon he didn't have before? Give him the weapon and fix it in the mix. Does the villain need some kind of power that hasn't been foreshadowed? Let her have the power and fix it in the mix.

While I don't recommend purposefully forgetting every spelling and grammar rule you've ever learned, and while you should try your best to tell the story without as many plot holes or weird, sudden character and tone shifts as possible, in the initial draft letting those things slide and fixing them later is perfectly acceptable.

This, to me, is freeing. It doesn't have to be perfect? I can write what I want? Sweet!

What To Do With Strong Characters, Ideas, or Scenes In Failed Work

I still think it's funny that John Fogerty was sued for plagiarizing himself. For those unfamiliar with the case, his former bandmates in Credence Clearwater Revival argued that the riff he wrote for "The Old Man Down the Road," a song from his solo album, *Centerfield*, sounded too close to the riff he wrote for "Run Through the Jungle," a song from CCR's *Cosmo's Factory*. The case went all the way to the Supreme Court, which ruled that it is not illegal for someone to sound too much like himself. It sounds like something straight out of *Catch-22*.

My point is that you are allowed to steal ideas from yourself. I strongly recommend it.

Salvage the good from the bad

I've mentioned my struggles with past projects, specifically *Igor's Inn*. While nearly every aspect of that novel didn't work, one idea, making my main characters participate in some kind of death-sport competition, stuck. I called it The Gauntlet. The games are admittedly silly. There is a rock climbing event during which little homunculi (including the one from *Raleigh's Prep*) attack the competitors, and there is some kind of gladiatorial Battle Royale. The final competition is a race that forces the competitors to outrun a group of townspeople armed with a variety of axes, shovels, pitchforks, clubs, bats, machetes, and other blunt instruments. If they catch any of the participants, well . . . .

Topher and his friends end up winning the race, and as a prize, they're carried back to the hotel they're staying in (Igor's Inn, of course), down an endless flight of stairs, and into Hell.

I liked The Gauntlet so much that I transformed it into the penultimate scene in *Burn All The Bodies*, the final book in the Topher Trilogy.

Recycling the good into the good

Many of my favorite authors like to connect the worlds they've created in separate novels, sometimes to great effect, sometimes to not-so-great effect. Stephen King does this. He has revisited Derry, Maine (from *IT*), and characters and events from one story or novel pop up in another. Captain Trips first shows up in the short story "Night Surf" from *Night Shift*; later it figures prominently in the novel *The Stand*. He attempted to blur the lines between all his books in his Dark Tower series by adding Randall Flagg (from *The Stand*) to the plot, even going so far as to rewrite the end of *The Stand* to make it work.

David Mitchell also connects his worlds. *Cloud Atlas* is filled with crossover characters and easter eggs, at least one of whom shows up in *Black Swan Green*. He also connected the world of *The Bone Clocks* (a novel I didn't like) to nearly every book he's written so far, then wrote *Slade House* (a novella I loved) set in the world of *The Bone Clocks*. His meta-references, because he planned them or because of serendipity, work well.

The challenge in recycling good ideas, plots, or characters, is to make it feel organic, to intertwine them in a way that doesn't make them seem like throw-away references, to use them for a reason that forwards the plot or has more meaning than just reference for reference sake.

So what's my point? I have two:

1. Don't give up on good ideas just because they didn't work the first time around. Being an author requires persistence, and persistence isn't defined only by seeing a project to completion but by harvesting everything you create, even if the initial yield wasn't all that great.

2. If it makes sense, let your characters, plots, and events intermingle from one book to the other. Steal from yourself! Even the Supreme Court says it's okay.

Reanimate your dead darlings

There's a quote floating around on the Internet from a "well-known literary agent" that states something like "I often find that a story begins on about page fifty," implying that most early drafts of any manuscript could stand to cut about 12,000 words from the beginning.

That might sound like a lot. Cutting 12,000 words is like cutting two weeks' worth of work! But the idea works pretty well. In hindsight, I usually get to the point where I'm ready to cut that much a little bit at a time. Sometimes it's in the second development draft, sometimes it's in the fourth. The first time I actively thought about doing something like that was about seven years ago when writing the early drafts of what eventually became *Bonesaw*, which itself inspired *The Rabbit, The Jaguar, & The Snake*. After the fourth or fifth time of slogging through about twenty pages of exposition, I realized that I had to get rid of them. I could either spread that information throughout the rest of the text or cut it completely. So I did, and the book quickly worked much better.

I did the same thing with "The Unan." The story started with three scenes that essentially explained how and why the three main characters, an old man and two children, ended up on the run in a jungle on a distant, unsettled planet. It was around draft four that I knew the section, however much I liked it, didn't fit into the narrative, so I axed it and started the story with the trio entering the jungle for the first time. It didn't just improve the pacing, it added a layer of mystery and suspense as well as some gray areas that I never answer.

The good news all of those dead darlings don't have to be buried. They can be reused, too. I ended up repackaging the section of "The Unan", titled it "The Blood Plague," and released it as a new short story. I did the same thing to some darlings that I dispatched from the second draft of *The Rabbit, The Jaguar, & The Snake*, repackaging them as *Scenes From The City* and releasing them as freebies to send to my email list. I produced them as print versions and either sell them at live events or use them as calls to action in other works. Since they're so short, I'll produce audiobook versions, too.

Your ideas are your ideas! Finding a way to maximize them is exactly what it means to be indie: be experimental, be entrepreneurial.

More Case Studies

Jason Riddle

Jason Riddle is a character that first appeared in "Under the Rocks," which I refer to as my "Rappahannock River Monster" short story. Here's the blurb:

Something evil is swimming in the waters of the Rappahannock River. Jason Riddle knows it. He and his brothers thought they killed it in the summer of 1932. Seventy years later, that evil has returned, and Riddle must destroy it once and for all.

However, before I published it in *A Knife in the Back*, I couldn't find a rhythm for the story. It contained way too much exposition, and I couldn't nail down a satisfactory ending, so I put it on the back burner while I worked on *Tracker's Travail*, the sequel to my first novel, *Raleigh's Prep*. Since *Tracker's Travail* was set in Fredericksburg, and I didn't know if "Under the Rocks" would ever work, I decided to steal one of my favorite characters from the short story and put it in the novel, only with a twist. In his first iteration, Riddle—a strong-willed septuagenarian with a biting sense of humor—was the hero hunting the monster; in the second, he's the monster hunting the hero.

The funny thing is that after I finished *Tracker's Travail*, I came up with a great ending for "Under the Rocks," but rather than change either story, I left them the way they were. I published the latter as the seventh short story in *A Knife in the Back* and pumped up Riddle's role in *Tracker's Travail*.

The Unnamed Protagonist from "The Unholy Triumvirate"

Sometimes writers come up with characters that stick with them, characters that, for some reason or another, beg to be delved into more deeply than originally intended. That's what happened with the main character of "The Unholy Triumvirate." He's one of the most profane characters I've ever written, but he's funny and oddly vulnerable. When I was casting around for ideas for a new novel after I finished *Burn All The Bodies*, he kept coming to mind. I'd like to say that I struggled with the premise, but that's not the case. It just came to me: put a gangster from 1920s NYC in a sci-fi/horror novel set after The Singularity and see what happens. The result was *Bonesaw*, a novel I didn't intend to be a part of a series. But after some excellent feedback from a beta reader, I decided to raise the stakes, explore the world I created, and write a trilogy. So the first book became the last, and I wrote *The Rabbit, The Jaguar, & The Snake*. Here's the blurb:

From the author of *A Knife in the Back*, *You Will Be Safe Here*, and *Burn All The Bodies* comes *The Rabbit, The Jaguar, & The Snake*, the first book in an epic series of adventure and survival.

When Bonesaw, an early 20th-century gangster, is rescued from prison by the Brotherhood, he doesn't realize it is a kidnapping. They need him to spy on one of their generals, and to do so he has to go through their version of Basic Training, also known as The Gauntlet (Golgotha,

Hell, and The Battle Royale). His choice is simple: do what they say or they'll cut off his head.

Nearly a century later, Detective Katherine Wheeler investigates a string of murders with similar, horrifying details: each victim dies when something huge erupts out of their bodies. Unbeknownst to her, the attacks are the beginning of an invasion, one that could wipe out all of Mankind.

Finally, deep in the jungle of a primitive planet, Coatl faces his most dangerous foe yet: the monstrous tecuani. When they overrun the last stronghold in the empire, he decides that the world has one last hope for survival: Ka-Bata and his army. But no one has seen Ka-Bata in years, and nobody even knows if he's still alive.

Separated by time and space, these three unlikely allies, The Rabbit, The Jaguar, and The Snake, must find a way to join forces. If they can, the human race has a chance to survive. If they can't, it is doomed.

(Yep. I revisited The Gauntlet. After I realized that I'd done it again, I promised myself that that was the last time.)

Mistress Chainwrought

Mistress Chainwrought is mentioned a few times in *Raleigh's Prep*. She's the evil headmaster responsible for the creation of the beasts that live in the woods surrounding the school, the monsters that simultaneously watch over the grounds and periodically kill the students. As a part of the mythology of the book, I always intended to tell her story, but since she existed before the three protagonists (Topher and crew), and since I couldn't figure out a way to write a story at the school without them in it, I never gave it a shot.

Until recently.

While writing the rough draft of *The Rabbit, The Jaguar, & The Snake*, I came up with a huge section that delved into her time at Raleigh's Prep and somehow connects to the new book. Her section didn't make it into *The Rabbit, The Jaguar, & The Snake*, but there's a strong chance she'll make it into the sequel, *Blood & Gold*. The fun part will be exploring an evil character from my first series and entwine her into the world of my second series. And even if she doesn't make the cut, I'll find a way to turn that work into something that can stand alone, or maybe I'll just turn it into a novel or novella.

On Audiobooks

There is a lot of noise in the self-publishing world about audiobooks right now. Book lovers are downloading them in ever-increasing amounts (in 2017, there was a 12% increase, and in 2018 there was a 4.6% increase over the 2017 numbers), and many indie icons—such as Joanna Penn and Jane Friedman—credit the use of smart devices (phones, Echo, and Home) with the rise.

Audiobooks?! I have NO idea how to do that

There are plenty of audiobook production services out there, but it can be quite expensive to use them. Fortunately, now it is easier than ever to do it yourself. Some people just use the Voice Message app on their phones, but I wouldn't recommend that. If all you're interested in doing is producing some good-quality marketing material, buy a large diaphragm microphone and download a free recording app such as Audacity. Windows PCs don't come with anything useful, but Mac users have Garageband, and it's simple to use.

I've been involved in music and video for a while, and since I already have all the gear and tech experience, turning my books into audio was a pretty easy decision to make. And while it's a lot of work (I have a full-time job, so it takes about two months for me to produce 30k words of audio), I love the whole process.

Here are some tricks and tips to get started producing an audiobook.

Preparation and Performance

1. Get your gear.

You'll need a large diaphragm microphone, a pop filter (or two), a mic stand, and a DAW (Digital Audio Workstation). I use a Blue Bluebird mic and Pro Tools. The mic was a little expensive ($299), and I pay for a yearly Pro Tools subscription ($199/year), but you don't even need to go to that extent. I've seen people record audiobooks on Audacity (Audacity is free), and there are a lot of affordable large-diaphragm mics out there. The AT2020 is only $82-$100.

2. Carve out a space.

Technology has made it possible to make a fairly decent recording in your house. Here's a picture of my little studio (Studio X!) in the house I'm renting right now:

It's not Sound City, but it works!

While you don't need a dedicated sound booth or an expensive studio to record anymore, you do need a place that won't echo or pick up too much room or outside noise. I've seen authors throw blankets over their computers to dampen sound or set up in closets. Avoid completely square rooms with lots of reflective surfaces. Turn off the AC or Heat while reading, as well as anything else that will create any noise (washers, dryers, dishwashers, fans, etc . . .)

3. Clean your power.

Sometimes the electricity will create an unwanted buzzing sound in your mic. You can buy a pretty inexpensive power conditioner to help get rid of buzz and hum. If you have access to Adobe Audition, use its Noise Reducer to get rid of it after recording, but it's always better to record as clean as you can.

4. It's a performance, so be a performer.

Many authors have a hard time performing their work. I've been to readings where the writer merely read directly from the page with a not-quite-monotone and not-at-all-engaging delivery. That's not fun to listen to. Give your characters a voice. Make it sound the way you'd want an actor to perform the role on stage. One side note: my brother recently told me he was listening to an audiobook where the male narrator broke into falsetto anytime he was reading the female character's dialog. Maybe it's subjective, but something like that would pop me out of the narrative. When I read a female character's voice, I might lighten up on my bass or soften my tone, but going into a falsetto is a little silly.

5. Get ready to work.

I can read about 5,000 words an hour before I tap out. Sometimes I can do more, sometimes I do less. (I teach full-time, so I don't have the energy to do more, but even if I did, I think I'd only be able to focus on two hours of narration at a time.) For an 88,000-word novel, it takes me about two weeks to record the audio.

Also, you'll be surprised at how many mistakes you make—mispronunciations, stumbling over syllables, slurs—not to mention the weird noises your nose, tongue, and mouth make. Once you get into a rhythm, the reading goes by faster, but don't be afraid to re-record something if the mic picks up a strange noise, or if you didn't pronounce something the way you wanted to pronounce it, or anything else that needs another take.

Okay, you've spent hours recording your audiobook, and now all you have to do is send it out as an MP3, right? Not quite. There are at least two more steps you need to complete before your masterpiece is ready to . . . move on to the final (I promise) step.

Editing & Processing

Before I get into the details of this part of the process, it is important to understand a few definitions and descriptions of the applications you can use.

Destructive Editing vs. Non-destructive Editing

Destructive editing changes the audio file you're working with immediately. While it's possible to undo changes, it's a pain to continually have to do that.

Non-destructive editing changes the audio file you're working with virtually. Undoing changes are much easier.

Some DAWs are only capable of destructive editing (like Audacity). Some are capable of non-destructive editing (like Logic, Audition (in Multi-track mode), and Pro-Tools). I use Pro-Tools for this reason.

1. Editing

Editing is probably the most tedious part of the whole process. It requires the editor to cut out as many weird breaths and pops and clicks caught in the recording. He also has to pull sections of audio apart, or squeeze them closer together to create more of a natural rhythm, or re-record sections that don't sound the way they should, or cut sections that might not work.

On breaths: cut out the breath before the beginning of a sentence. Reduce the volume of a breath in the middle of a sentence. If a breath creates tone, keep it and reduce it. If cutting it makes the audio sound weird, keep it and reduce it. Otherwise, cut.

On room tone, clicks, and pops: Unfortunately, you probably don't have a treated room, so there will be room tone (the nearly imperceptible white noise of the air and the space in the room where you're recording.) In addition, clicking and popping happen when we speak. You'll need to try to get rid of as many of these as possible.

Fortunately, there is a DAW you can employ to reduce or eradicate nearly all of those problems: Adobe Audition. Learn to use the Noise Reduction tool to get rid of the room tone.

Use iZotope Rx7 to get rid of clicking and popping.

Editing is time-consuming, to say the least. Count on spending at least an hour editing each five to ten-minute section of audio. Here's how that works out for me:

If one chapter = 5,000 words and 5,000 words = roughly 30 minutes of audio, it takes me approximately 3-6 hours to edit one chapter. *The Rabbit, The Jaguar, & The Snake*, which I'm going to produce soon, is 22 chapters long. So it will take me about 66 to 132 hours to edit that audiobook.

Yeah, I am a slow audio editor.

It's my least favorite part of the process. I only edit an hour at a time, and I only work in twenty-minute chunks (with a ten-minute break in between). Sometimes I get into a rhythm and knock out fifteen minutes of recorded audio in an hour. Sometimes I get eight or nine. Sometimes I put twenty minutes in and I'm done.

2. Processing

There are a ton of technical steps that audio engineers take when mixing multitrack sessions (multitrack means multiple tracks of sound—two guitars, a bass, vocals, 9-12 drum mics). Audiobooks probably have one mono or stereo track. That's not to say multi-tracking isn't possible. It is. I multi-track when adding effects to my characters' voices (like delay or pitch shifting). Processing a single audio track is always easier, though. While there are more advanced methods of increasing the quality of the recording (such as adding effects and analog warmth), the first two things to master are EQ and Compression.

EQ

This stands for Equalization. The easy description of EQ is this: EQ contains the frequency ranges of sound, from bass frequencies to high frequencies. The best practice for EQ is to reduce rather than add. For example, I cut the bass below 40ish hz and add a little air at 12 kHz. I also take a little out in the mid-range, somewhere between 500 to 1khz. Adding or cutting too much (for me, that's more than 3dbs) will probably result in less than desirable sound.

Compression

When you read, you'll notice that the loudness of your voice will go up and down. To keep the volume even, add compression. Many DAWs have template settings that fit your recording. My advice is to make sure not to squash your voice. Make sure to compress it at a 2:1 ratio and don't reduce it more than 3dbs.

Mastering

The final step in audiobook production is to make sure the files meet the loudness requirements of the hosts that will sell your book.

Find your DAW's Limiter

A limiter will bring the volume of your track up to an acceptable level for consumers. Check with your distributor's requirements to know what that level is. ACX/Audible requires that it be no louder than -3 db, and even though I use Findaway Voices to distribute my audiobooks, I set the Ceiling at -3 db so I can avoid any issues with Audible.

The limiter I use in Pro Tools is Maxim.

1. Set the Ceiling at -1db

2. Line up a professionally produced audiobook as a reference and play it simultaneously with your audiobook.

3. Adjust the Threshold until the two are the same volume.

4. Let the audiobooks play for at least a minute or two and keep an eye on the Attenuation. If it goes over 3 dB, adjust the Threshold until it doesn't do that anymore.

5. Commit your track.

iZotope also has an AI application called Ozone that will master your work fairly well, too. You need to have some audio knowledge to make it work properly, but if you're not afraid to push some buttons and learn form some YouTube tutorials, I recommend using it.

Distribution

The audiobook is done! Now . . . how do you get it out to your readers/listeners?

I'm old enough to remember checking out audiobooks on cassette tape from my library. They had those super-clunky, smoked plastic cases, and they were well-used. Buying one never seemed to be an option for me because of the massive amount of tapes, although the move to CDs made it a little easier. Now, however, anybody can download an entire five to six-hour audiobook onto a mobile device in minutes. That makes it easier for indie authors to reach a wider audience with a variety of mediums. As an author, I've used four different distribution methods. Here they are in order of preference/usefulness:

1. Findaway Voices

I discovered Findaway Voices through Draft2Digital. All you have to do is upload your audio and complete the description information, and Findaway sends it out to over twenty-four different online stores all over the world. This includes Audible (the most popular place to download audiobooks). However, I've found that I make the most money from licensing my audiobooks to libraries, and Findaway Voices distributes to Overdrive and Bibliotheca and other services that loan my audiobooks out to patrons. I can price the audiobooks any way I want, and I can change anything in the listing (from audio to pricing) once every thirty days. The split is what it is. I'm paying for distribution with over 50% of my sales. I don't like it, but that's the best way to build an audience at this point (for me, at least).

2. Put it up on your website

I only do this so I can have a store that I control on my own. That way if a service goes down, I'll always have my material up to sell. Also, instead of driving traffic to another site with my ad buys, I can use my content to drive people to my site. I make 100% of the profits from this method. Until I can afford to do massive audiobook ad buys, my distribution is weak. And by that, I mean non-existent.

3. Start a podcast

I use Buzzsprout to upload my audiobooks to Spotify, iTunes, Google Play, and other services. This equates to giving away content for free, but it's evergreen marketing, and you can set up a Patreon to earn money through crowdfunding.

On ACX Exchange

This is the author portal for Audible. I started here before moving over to Findaway Voices. I found the customer service poor, the contract overly restrictive (7 years! Are you kidding me?), and the results lackluster. The split isn't good enough, either, although they have raised the percentage I earn recently, (maybe because of the competition from Findaway Voices?). I don't recommend going this route. You can also distribute it to Audible through Findaway Voices! So there's no reason to sign an exclusive contract.

Part II Top Five Takeaways

1. Planner, Pantser, or Plantser? Decide on which brainstorming and pre-writing process fits best.

2. Popular fiction often uses some kind of structure, so if you want to write that kind of story, use one of the popular structures.

3. The first draft is not going to be perfect, nor should it be. Don't let perfectionism get in the way of writing something good.

4. Don't skimp on Development, Line, and Copy editing. Nobody wants to read something that isn't well-edited. Consider finding a professional editor.

5. You can't self-plagiarize, so reuse strong plots, scenes, and characters from failed work.

Bonus Takeaway!

Consider learning how to produce audiobooks. Not only is it a growing part of the book industry, but it helps with the editing process.

PART III: MARKETING FOR BEGINNERS

After I published *Burn All The Bodies*, I scheduled three weekends with my local library system (the Central Rappahannock Regional Library) to set up my table and sell my books. From what I understand, because the CRRL covers two counties and a city, authors are allowed to make sales at events the system holds. It went fairly well, as well as can be expected for trying to sell books at a place where people go to check books out for free. On the last day, a man approached me and asked questions about my books, how long I'd been writing, etc. He told me that he, too, wrote novels but wasn't able to find an agent.

"That's hard to do," I said. "It's the reason why I decided to do it myself."

"Does what you're doing here work?"

"A little bit. Not as well as I'd hoped. I'm going to have to adjust my tactics."

"Yeah. I'd self-publish, too but I don't want to do any of this kind of thing. I just want to write."

I understand this position. For a long time, that's all I wanted to do, too. It's the traditional way of publishing.

Leave the creation to the creatives and the business to the business people. Unfortunately, this isn't true anymore for people who are traditionally published. There is only so much effort a publisher will put into marketing new and mid-level authors, and unless you're A-list talent, you're going to have to learn how to market your work anyway. Why? It's not worth their time and money. They take the same approach many indie authors who are not marketing-oriented take. They press the publish button and hope by existing the book will find an audience.

Authors who want to be traditionally published to take advantage of a publishing house's marketing engine might want to rethink that strategy. Many publishers are looking for authors who already have:

- established a marketing platform.

- gathered a following.

- set up an email list that can reach their readers directly.

Even if you've done all that, even if you've worked with Amazon Ads and Facebook Ads, traveled around and sold your books at events, and built a 1000+ email list, traditional publishers still want their authors to market on their own.

The following section is for anybody who has never marketed a book before. In it, I will describe how I started marking and recount my failures and successes.

What Has Not Worked For Me

If you're anything like I was when I finished my first series, you're confident that the material is worth an audience but have no idea how to find one. For three years after I published my first book, *A Knife in the Back*, I cast around for ways to get it into the hands of readers. Most of the time I felt like I was just spinning my wheels. Here's a list of the things I did to attempt to market my work:

1. Ran Goodreads giveaways.
2. Ran freebies on KDP.
3. Held local readings.
4. Used Facebook to post about my work.
5. Gave copies to my local library system.

Unsurprisingly, this kind of scattershot approach didn't work. Other than some freebie winners and a few intrepid Amazon buyers, I sold a grand total of Very Little to Not At All.

I'd always known that I needed to learn about book marketing, but I just couldn't get past the feeling that I'd be pushing my work on people who didn't want to be sold to.

It felt synonymous with taking someone's money. It felt gross and slimy. But there is a difference between selling people something they don't want and marketing to them. The turn began when, after doing some research, I learned that marketing is letting people know what I was up to creatively.

That's it.

No pressure techniques. No scheming. No smarminess. There are people out there who like to read the kinds of stories I write (horror and sci-fi). I'm one of them. I know tons of them. I don't mind at all when someone who has written a book that I might like tells me about it, so why would I be worried about telling someone I wrote a book they might like? Marketing is more "Do you like reading cool stuff?" and less "Psst, buddy. Wanna buy something?"

Before I get started recounting my own experiences with marketing, I learned a lot of these tactics by reading these four books:

Your First 1,000 Copies, by Tim Grahl

Write. Publish. Repeat. by Sean Platt, Johnny B. Truant, and David Wright

Permission Marketing, by Seth Godin

How To Market Your Book, by Joanna Penn

In the past year, I've also gotten a lot out of listening to their podcasts:

The Self-Publishing Podcast (Johnny, Sean, and Dave)

The Creative Penn (Joanna Penn)

The Book Launch Show (Tim Grahl)

I strongly recommend reading these books and listening to these podcasts. They helped me overcome the first hurdle (that marketing is slimy), the second hurdle (the imposter syndrome), and have continued to provide valuable advice as I continue to build my fanbase and create my brand. Even more importantly, they provide simple, practical, actionable tips for getting started fast.

In this section, I'm going to explain how I applied their advice, techniques, strategies, and tactics, and recount my experience with it all so far—what I've done wrong, what I've done right, what I added, and what I made up myself.

Bring Your Work To The People Who Want To Read It

This might sound obvious, but the reason your book isn't selling is that nobody knows about it. So bring it to them. Here's a tactic I got from Tim Grahl's book. Since I write horror, post-apocalyptic, and science fiction, the first thing I did when I started to seriously market my books was to sign up for as many shows, festivals, and comic and horror conventions as I could afford.

Depending on the convention, it can be expensive. On average, I pay $100 per table per day, which means most one-day conventions will cost $100, and most three-day conventions will cost about $300. Larger, more established shows will cost more. Which leads me to a very important point:

DON'T GO INTO DEBT FOR THIS

Think about the numbers. If a vendor pays $100 for a table at a one-day event and sells her books for $10 each, she'll need to sell ten books to make her money back. But that doesn't include gas and food, so she should add about $50 to $75 to the bill. Now she'll have to sell fifteen to eighteen books to break even. Then she'll need to restock her books, which takes more out of her revenue. And pay taxes on sales, which takes even more.

If you're going to an out-of-town, multi-day event, you'll need to add lodging to your bill. Hotels are expensive, and Airbnb can be less, but it still makes it more difficult to break even. Going to live events, as much as I like it and as much as it works to establish a base-level readership and might create revenue, is not very profitable.

That's why I set marketing goals when I started doing this. Instead of looking at live events as the primary way I sell my books, I used them to establish a readership and an email list. My goal when I started was to sell 1,000 copies of my books and get a minimum of 500 people on my email list. It is a marketing investment, a short-term tactic, not at all a sustainable way of doing business, not unless I can triple my revenue.

Here is how I've done so far:

The first show I attended was The Gaithersburg Book Festival in February 2013. This was three years before I started seriously marketing. The table was only $100, and Gaithersburg is only an hour or so from where I live. It was rainy that day and I didn't sell very much, so I didn't have a high opinion of it. I was so turned off by the experience that I didn't attend another show for three years. In hindsight, I didn't do the work to prepare for it. I only had one book, I didn't decorate my table, and I didn't have an email sign-up. I wasn't ready.

Three years later, however, I'd done my homework. Since 2016, I've attended a lot more events where I could market my work, build my email list (and brand), and sell books. It's December 2017 at the time of this draft.

Here's a list of nearly all of the shows I've attended since I started in May 2016:

1. Awesome Con (Washington D.C.) 2016 and 2017
2. The VA Comic-Con (Richmond, VA) Two in 2016; Three in 2017
3. Heroes Con (Charlotte, NC) 2016
4. Art in the Park (Fredericksburg, VA) Six in 2016; Six in 2017
5. Scares that Care (Williamsburg, VA) 2016 and 2017
6. The Baltimore Comic-Con (Baltimore, MD) 2016
7. The Fredericksburg Independent Book Festival (Fredericksburg, VA) 2016 and 2017
8. The VA Comic Con Halloweekend (Richmond, VA) 2016
9. The Garfield Craft Show (Prince William County, Va) 2016
10. Alexandria Holiday Market (Alexandria, VA)
11. Oak City Comic Con (Raleigh, NC) 2017
12. Mars Con (Williamsburg, VA) 2017
13. The Greater Philadelphia Comicon (Philadelphia, PA) 2017
14. Roanoke Valley Comicon (Roanoke Valley, VA) 2017
15. The Tidewater Comicon (Va Beach, VA) 2017

16. The Gaithersburg Book Festival (Gaithersburg, MD) 2017

17. Balticon (Baltimore, MD) 2017

18. Rock the River (Fredericksburg, VA) 2017

19. Fred Con (Fredericksburg, VA) 2017

20. Conapalooza (Bristol, VA) 2017

21. Mistletoe Market (Fredericksburg, VA) 2017

22. The VA Comic Con Holiday Show (Richmond, VA) 2017

Here's what I've learned so far:

1. Sometimes I sell three to five books. Sometimes I sell twenty to forty.

2. If a lot of people attend, the amount I sell increases. There are, of course, outliers in that equation. I've sold well at low-attendance events and poorly at high-attendance events.

3. Sometimes I sell well because I'm the only author in attendance; sometimes I sell poorly because of bad table placement.

4. At comic cons, I'm one of maybe five or ten horror authors; at a horror con, I'm one of dozens.

5. I sell more illustrated short stories at literary events, and I sell more novels and non-illustrated work at comic cons.

6. It is very difficult to turn a profit as an author at larger events. A table can cost $200-$350, gas $33-$66, lodging $45-$500 (depending on whether I use Airbnb or a hotel), parking $16-$48, food per diem $30. My total cost for the weekend ends up being $386-$1,054.

7. The larger events can draw between up to 50,000 people. I might take a loss, and I can't always attend them because of that, or I might break even, but sales is a numbers game. The more people who walk by my table, the more sales I make. More people sign up for my email list. I hate the phrase "you're paid in exposure," but in this case, I consider it a marketing opportunity. I've built my list this way, and while I don't have huge numbers on it, I do have a list.

8. Three-day events are great, especially if they're run well. But they can be long and draining. Fridays seem to be a loss across the board. Even at Awesomecon 2017, where a lot of people showed up, Friday was slow. As someone in Artist's Alley, I'll meet a few nice people and make a few sales, but many of them are just browsing and chatting. Not a bad thing! Saturdays are generally the busiest days. Sundays are slightly better than Fridays, though I've had some Sundays that beat out my Saturdays in terms of sales and marketing.

9. One-day events are fine, too, but only if they're within a short driving distance. For me, driving to anything that takes over an hour might not be worth it. There are a lot of pros to attending one-day

events. They're generally more affordable, costing somewhere between $45-$100 per space. I don't attend any one-day events that cost more than $100. If you're like me and have a day job, you don't have to give up your whole weekend. I've attended some one-day events that ended up being more profitable than some of the three-day events.

10. On the flip side, setting everything up and tearing it all down again a few hours later is a chore, and since it only lasts one day, I get to market my work to fewer people.

11. I prefer two-day events, only because of the affordability and sweat equity. These tend to be held on Saturdays and Sundays. They cost around $175 to $200 per space. Yes, I end up spending my whole weekend selling books and marketing, but since I only attend those within an hour to an hour and a half driving range, I can still drive home if I choose and enjoy the evenings. All of the pros and cons of a Sunday event still apply, however. Most of the time if people come at all it's around lunchtime, and if it's clear that nobody is going to show up anymore, I've left more than a few an hour or so early.

I would recommend attending live events when you're just getting started. It's a great way to jumpstart your marketing engine, build an email list, and get your books, name, and brand out in front of people who might turn into readers and fans.

It's really easy to calculate the revenue, profit, and ROI, too. If an event is too far away and it's too difficult to break even, unless it provides amazing networking opportunities, I probably won't go back, at least not every subsequent year. If it's relatively close (within that hour-and-a-half window) and somewhat unprofitable, I still might attend, especially if attendance is high and there are plenty of networking opportunities. If it's close, profitable, and provides those opportunities, it's a lock for me to return.

I have no illusions about where I stand in terms of sales, revenue, profit, and ROI. Even after a year and a half, I feel like I'm still beginning. There are also people out there who are doing a lot better (in terms of ebook sales). But what's the alternative? Doing nothing. And doing nothing results in . . . nothing. There are close to one thousand people who have read or are about to read my books, people who, if I hadn't paid to attend these events, wouldn't have otherwise. These are people who will, if they become fans, either pick up the next book in my first completed series or pick up the first book in my next series—either at the next event I attend or online.

Even more importantly, I get to make a personal connection with the people who like to read the kinds of stories I write. It's pretty awesome to talk to these folks. They love reading, and they make it a point to come out and support indie-authors. What more could a beginning indie author ask for? Many are aspiring writers, too, and they ask me about writing, publishing, and marketing, which, of course, is something I'm happy to discuss. It was at one of these events (Mars Con) that I sold a book to Robin Abess, who left me this five-star review on Amazon:

> I bought this book at Marscon directly from Mr. Noll himself. I love the horror genre, and the book interested me. I truly enjoyed all the stories in the book. There are 7 short stories and a novella, plus

the beginning of another story with some of the same characters from the novella. I enjoyed all the stories, but a couple of my favorites were 'Beta', regarding a remote village being terrorized by...something in the woods, and 'Under the Rocks', which dealt with a river and the monster therein. The novella was different as well; interesting characters, quite a lot of death and gore, and some twists and turns.

I look forward to reading more of Mr. Noll's work in the future!

Thanks, Robin!

Never underestimate the power of engaging with readers and people who share your interests.

On Bad Reviews

Here is a negative review I received on Goodreads, whose reader-reviewers are notorious for giving brutal reviews.

I got about 25% in and I just can't finish it. The tough guy talk of the main character ranges anywhere from annoying to racist and the female lead isn't any better. If you're into hardboiled characters that don't take shit offa nobody (with a supernatural demonic type element), then maybe this is for you. It just wasn't my thing.

That one stung the first time I read it. But now it doesn't bother me. Somebody out there might read it and think, "I'm into hardboiled characters that don't take shit offa nobody" and buy the book.

One of the primary rules of the Writers' Workshop I teach is that during the feedback section, a writer is never allowed to try to explain something somebody didn't like. Here's how that applies to online reviews: Arguing with a critic is a waste of time. A note is a note. Take it or leave it.

Maximizing Your Live Event Experience

There are many approaches to live events that can ruin the experience. One surefire way to set yourself up for misery is to spend your time worrying about sales and/or comparing your sales to those of the vendors around you. Sales are important, (nobody should attend events where a lack of sales repeatedly puts the business in the red), but since marketing can be defined as "teaching the consumer why your product is better than others," that can also be your goal at a live event.

Host or Get On A Panel

Writers have more to offer than just writing. People are quite interested in the creative and marketing process. They love talking to writers about writing, where the ideas come from, how long it takes to write a novel, what self-publishers do to market their work.

Most of the entertainment-minded events (book festivals, comic cons) feature information sessions, panels, and author readings. Some of the panels I've sat in on were about "Quiet Horror—what is it and how is it achieved," "Adventures in Self-Publishing," and "The highs and lows of running a comic-con." These are perfect opportunities to market your work and your brand. The more well-organized events will do a few things with your participation:

- They'll put your name on the online schedule with links back to your website.
- They'll send out emails to their lists featuring your name and links back to your website.

- They'll post your bio and a link back to your webpage on social media.

- They'll create event invites and invite their extensive social media followers.

I've tracked traffic coming to my website from those kinds of tactics. The closer it gets to the day of the event, the more hits I get. That's free marketing.

Do I expect to make thousands of dollars in sales because of it all? Of course not. But I get to share my books and short stories with a wider audience, and the more opportunities I get to do that, the better. It's a long-game tactic: keep your name and your work in front of people, let them know what you're doing, make connections at live events, and get to know potential fans.

Panel and speaking opportunities can result in sales, too. After the panel on quiet horror, I sold a copy of *Burn All The Bodies* to someone who was in the audience. I also spoke to someone who runs a horror book group who asked if I'd be willing to come down and talk to the club after they read one of my books. She also invited me to set up my table at the haunted house she runs which has become a good event for me to market my work. After the panel on running comic cons, I sold books to people in the audience. All of them signed up for my email list, too.

I don't view marketing as a cut-throat enterprise. I don't want to stomp on my fellow writers, make enemies, or irritate people. I want to be a part of a community that loves reading and storytelling. A great way to do that is to get out in front of those people and talk about what I do.

Offer To Do Free Readings Or Talks At Local Venues

I'm fortunate to live in a town with a lot of different restaurants, coffee houses, and breweries, all of which are more than happy to partner up with local artists, musicians, and writers to host art shows, live music, and readings. It's a symbiotic relationship. The venue that hosts the event attracts customers, and the artist gets to market and sell his work for free. The venue offers food and drinks, and if the venue is located in a downtown area, it can turn into AN EVENT, something people look forward to attending.

Remember, nobody is alone in this. I don't mean that in the *Alien* "there are space creatures out there trying to kill you" way but more in the "there are probably other writers in your area" way. Organize a joint reading. Mix genres. Get a poet, a mystery writer, and a biographer, or a horror writer, a romance writer, and someone who writes contemporary literature. (Avoid the obvious mismatch of splatter-punk and children's books, of course.)

The purpose is to harness the power of your fans and supporters. By yourself, you'll nab five to ten friends and family members. With other authors, the number of audience members could go up to a solid thirty to forty.

Two Years of Events By The Numbers

Years Spent Live Marketing	1.7
Number of Events Attended	38
Number of Books Sold	756
Average Sold by Month	40
Average Sold by Event	20

After traveling to events for approximately two years, I began to cut down on those that were less successful and re-attending those that continue to be profitable. I also raised my prices. At first, I was selling my novels for $10 and my illustrated short stories for $5 (all three novels for $25; three illustrated short stories for $12). Now I charge $8 per illustrated short story (or three for $20), $20 per novel, $15 per serial release, and, depending on the length of the work, either $35 or $25 for complete collections.

The Fabled Email List

Every book I've read on book marketing overwhelmingly stresses the importance of regularly engaging your audience through email. The people on your list are interested in your work. They are not bothered by your emails. They asked to receive them. It's just another way of maintaining a relationship with someone from a live event or someone who bought your book online.

It takes a long time to build a list. I managed to get 450 in nineteen months; after three years, that number has risen to 948. It won't guarantee sudden blockbuster sales, (I have a 50% engagement rate), but there isn't any reason not to do it. It's simple to set up an automation, and it's free up to a certain amount of subscribers. The other option, not building it, results in nothing. That's the opposite of marketing.

The purpose of this section is to give you some tips for building an email list and recount my experience so far in building my own.

Quick Basics

Don't use Gmail. It's not set up for this kind of thing. Use a service like MailChimp, GetResponse, or Constant Contact. I use MailChimp. (Note—my mentioning of them here in no way constitutes an endorsement. As always, do your homework and find one that is best suited for your needs).

Put an email sign-up on your webpage.

Use a double-opt-in method.*

Keep all records of people who signed up for your list at a live event.*

(*The double-opt-in sends an email to someone signing up for your list to make sure they wanted to do it. Their opt-in is recorded and time-stamped. The live events list is also proof that someone wanted to receive emails from you.)

The Funnel

The idea of an email marketing funnel might be new to you, but it's something marketers have done forever to attract an audience and build a brand. The idea behind the funnel is to attract potential readers by giving her something free (a novel or short story or audiobook). Then if that reader likes it, she will be more likely to buy one of your other products. Your job is to create a scaled price ladder to steer the reader to more and more expensive items. Since we're talking about books here, it won't be like you're fleecing anybody Your most expensive novel will most likely cost between $15.00 and $20.00. Your most expensive print omnibus (or box set) might be $35.00 to $45.00. These numbers are lower if you're using digital copies. My ebook novels are $2.99 each, and my omnibus editions are $4.99 each.

That's a simplified version of the funnel. Here's one way I've used it. Sign up for my email list and get:

- A free digital copy of *Raleigh's Prep*. *Raleigh's Prep* is the first novel in my Topher Trilogy.

- Using my MailChimp automation, anybody who downloads *Raleigh's Prep* will have a free first chapter of the second novel in the series, *Tracker's Travail*, sent to them in their email.

- Anybody who downloads that will be sent an offer to buy *Tracker's Travail* for $0.99.

Another way works like this:

- Send a digital version of one of my illustrated short stories to my list for free.

- A free chapter of *Raleigh's Prep* follows the story.

- I put a Call To Action for *Mad Tales*, the omnibus edition of all three books in my first series, at the end. Sixteen short stories and three novels. Only $4.99 for a digital copy.

Here's one last example:

- Send a free illustrated short story to my email list.

- Anybody who downloads it receives an email for a discount on a Basic Customized Short Story (it's a tiered service I offer) which is set in the same world as the free short story.

- Anybody who clicks on the discount offer receives an email offering a discount on a Premium Customized short story.

Books aren't like art or music, both of which a potential fan can sample by actually looking at a painting or illustration or listening to a song. At an event, the risk a reader takes buying a book based on how much they like the genre, a blurb, and the fact that they came there to spend money, sharing something for free goes a long way to assuage any discomfort he might feel.

Interesting note: Offering your audience all of these options, in addition to keeping them up to date with all of the cool things you're doing, provides information. Since I write horror and science fiction, I get to understand which portion of my list likes which genre. Since I attend a lot of events, I get to know who is interested in going to them. And since I offer a lot of other content and services (Customized Short Stories, Original Music, Writing Coaching, Freelance Writing, and Editing), I can track who might be interested in those services and target my emails towards those individuals.

"But won't I bother people with all of my emails?"

Short answer: no. They signed up for your newsletter. If they no longer want to receive them, they can always easily unsubscribe.

Slightly longer answer: Remember that marketing isn't slimy salesmanship. It's letting a group of people who are interested in what you do and that you have something new to offer. That's it.

Counter-argument for balance: yes, but only if you bombard them with emails. One every week is enough.

Your readers want a new book. You've written a new book. Your email can say, "Hey, I wrote a new book! You read one of my other books. Maybe you'll like this one." Or it can say, "Hi there! Thank you for buying my book(s). Here are the other books I have that you might like, too."

"How Do I Get People To Sign Up For My List?"

Here's what doesn't work: putting a sign-up on a website or social media page and expecting people to find it by themselves.

You need to show up.

I put an email sign-up sheet out at every live event I attend. If someone buys my book, I ask them to sign up. If someone reads my blurb but doesn't want to buy anything, I tell them they can get a free story if they sign up for the list.

Facebook ads also work. I've run two ads in the last year, paid $300, and netted 150 new subscribers.

There are a lot of offers out there that claim to be able to grow your list into the thousands "with this one, simple trick," but that sounds like a gimmick to me. I'd rather build my list one person at a time. That way I know the people who receive my emails are truly interested in what I have to say.

Some Practicalities of Email Marketing, and How I Adjusted After The First Year

As someone new to marketing, trying to balance productivity, going to live events, maintaining some kind of social media presence, learning about ads, learning about the funnel, and coming up with an email marketing strategy can be overwhelming.

The automated string of emails I've set up reduces some of the pressure to produce newsletters and offers every week.

Automation is exactly what it sounds like: a set of emails that are scheduled to be sent to your email list. It gets much more complicated than that, with sub-campaigns, if/then charts, segmentation, and re-targeting, but for starters, setting up an easy string will suffice.

Mine starts with a "Welcome To My List" email, which includes a free novel, audiobook, and theme song. After that, I set the automation to send an email every two weeks for a year. The first email contains what amounts to a blog post. I talk about my work and writing in general. The second email contains a simple Call To Action (did you read *A Knife in the Back*? You'll love the sequel!).

What Else Can I Send?

One-off campaigns work, too. It's always a great idea to let your list know about the new/cool things you're up to. Are you vending or speaking at an event nearby? Send an email to people on your list who live within a certain radius of the venue. Do you offer any neat or interesting services your readers might like? Send them information about it.

For example, when I attended Heroes.con, I noticed that the artist next to me did a lot of business selling commissions. He drew caricatures and fan art and inserted his customers' faces onto drawings of their favorite superheroes. I decided to offer the same thing, only since I'm not an artist, I did it with short stories.

Thus, my Customized Short Story Service was born. The idea is simple: pick one of my templates—Zombie, Post-Apocalyptic Death Cult, Rappahannock River Monster, Be the Murderer, Post-Apocalyptic Sci-fi Adventure, YA Sci-fi Adventure, or Alien Invasion. Choose whether you want to live or die. Then choose your level. I have four: Basic, Premium, Deluxe, and Super-Deluxe. For the Basic level, I'll put your name into the story. The Premium level requires that you provide three details that I have to somehow work into the story. I had one customer ask for a bottle of mustard, kittens, and a plane crash into the Rappahannock River Monster story. Another wanted his friend to die in the first scene of the Post-Apocalyptic Death Cult story. I also had to figure out how to include

Weird Al Yankovich and the Borg. At the Deluxe level, customers get everything from the Premium level plus an audiobook version of the story, and at the Super-Deluxe level, customers get everything at the Deluxe level plus an original song.

Why four levels? To employ the psychology of the consumer. What I want people to do is buy the Premium level. It has the best ROI and takes the least amount of time to produce. By giving a customer a less expensive option and two more expensive options, consumers are attracted to the more reasonably priced middle-ground.

Use Cut Chapters and Outtakes

Remember the section about recycling your work? I use that stuff for marketing purposes as well. Throughout the drafting of everything I've written, I've cut scenes, chapters, and entire sections along the way to the final draft. Some of them are dead. There's no reason to resurrect them for any purpose. But some of them are good, and the only reason I cut them was that they didn't serve the larger work. They usually work well as pieces of flash fiction, but some of the longer excerpts can be turned into short stories. They can function as freebies to your list, teasers for an upcoming release, or as bonus items for a book launch. Send them off as .mobi, .epub, and .pdfs. Turn them into audiobooks. Track who clicks on them, and retarget for the launch of future releases. Eventually, there will be enough material to release as a separate work.

Use Your Other Creative Pursuits To Create Content

Many writers, from newbies to grizzled vets, have plenty of written content to use for funnel marketing. Use the same idea to create content in other mediums, too. Are you an artist or a musician? Do you take photographs, or create sculptures? If there is a way to incorporate the other creative things you do into your writing, do it.

I'm a musician, so produce theme music for all of the short stories and novels I write. Since I have the gear, I also produce audiobook versions of everything I write. Sometimes I give a song or a short story audiobook away as a marketing tool.

By doing this, I create a brand and a body of work. The more avenues I can create to bring future fans to my books, the better. The more intellectual property I create, the better.

Reviewing The First Year

I started my email list on May 14, 2016. As of December 21, 2017, my list grew from zero to 452. It would be close to five hundred, but I've had forty-one unsubscribes. As of that same date, here is the data regarding opens and clicks for the entire automation:

667 opens; 81 clicks.

Here are the numbers regarding my first email, the one with all the freebies:

Sent: 556

Total Opens: 43.7% (247)

Clicks per Unique Opens: 19.2% (111)

Here's a breakdown of how many people clicked on which freebie:

Title	Total Clicks	Unique Clicks
"Beta" (a short story) .pdf	22 (20%)	18 (22%)
"Beta's Tune" (theme music)	15 (14%)	12 (14%)
"Beta" (a short story) .epub	11 (10%)	3 (4%)
"Beta" (audiobook)	5 (5%)	3 (4%)

Here are the Industry Averages:

Open Rate: 22.4%
Click Rate: 2.7%

These numbers don't include data from the other twenty or so emails I sent in the first year. I did notice that the CTA I sent out every other week, the emails that just advertised a book, did not earn high open and click rates. I also noticed that while open and click rates varied, the further down the email trail a subscriber was, the less they opened and clicked. While this kind of email fatigue is often the case, I do need to come up with strategies to re-engage my audience.

Dealing with List Fatigue: Revamp and Revise

First, I created a Primary Automation. The Primary Automation contains six emails, starting with Email 1: Welcome To My List! (with all of the freebies) and Email 2: Introducing My Customized Short Stories. Email 3 was written to announce whatever new novel I'm working on at the time. In 2017 it was *The Rabbit, The Jaguar, & The Snake*. In 2018 it was *The Hive*. In 2019, The Wounded, The Sick, & The Dead. In 2020 it will be this book! Then the sequel to *The Rabbit, The Jaguar, & The Snake: Blood & Gold*. Email four markets the audiobooks I've produced and emails five and six contain reviews of my favorite books.

Second, I created several sub-automations that are triggered by the subscriber's behavior. Because of the options MailChimp affords, these automations can be complex, but it comes down to creating a series of "if/then" triggers. Here's what I'm talking about using email three as an example:

1. Two weeks after the final email in the primary automation is sent, a subscriber who opens the second email will be sent a Free First Chapter email.

2. If a subscriber clicks on the Free First Chapter link, then three days later, he or she will be sent an offer to buy the book.

3. If a subscriber clicks on any link in the prior email, then one week later he or she will be sent an email with a thank you and a free outtake from *The Rabbit, The Jaguar, & The Snake*. Included in that email will be another chance for the subscriber to buy the book (just in case they haven't yet).

4. If a subscriber is sent but doesn't open the primary list email, then one week later they'll be sent a Free First Chapter email.

5. If a subscriber clicks on the Free First Chapter link, then three days later, he or she will be sent an offer to buy the book.

6. If a subscriber clicks on any link in the prior email, then one week later he or she will be sent an email with a thank you and a free outtake from *The Rabbit, The Jaguar, & The Snake*. Included in that email will be another chance for the subscriber to buy the book (just in case they haven't, yet).

If you're a visual learner, turn the page for a flowchart:

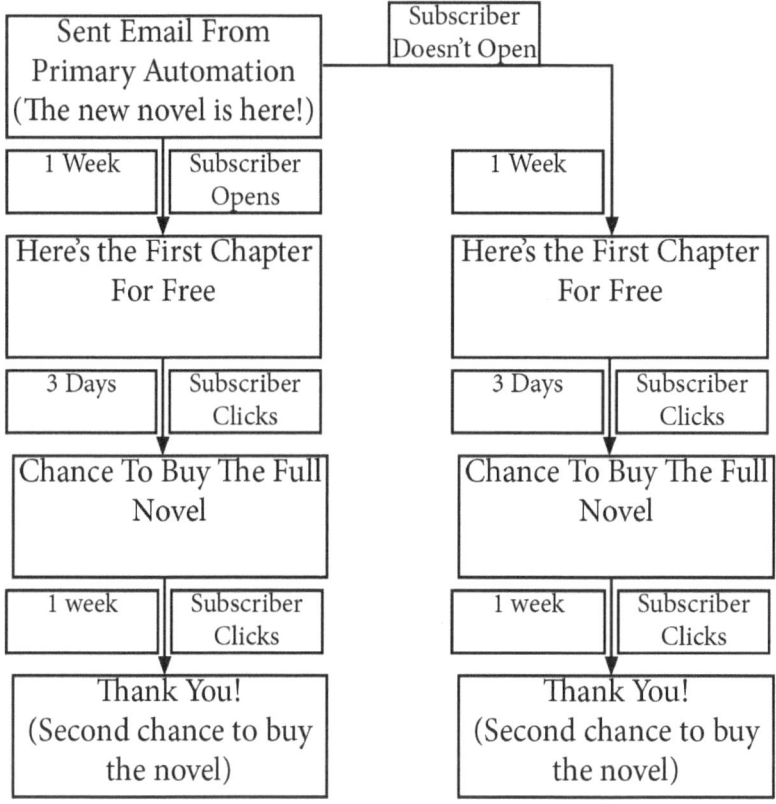

Notice that I'm not trying to hard-sell anybody. The emails are based on behavior. If a subscriber is interested enough to open or click on something, the automation responds. If they're not, a retarget is as aggressive as I get.

I look at email marketing as a way of keeping up with anybody I met out on the road who was kind enough to buy one of my books. If it results in a sale, awesome. If all it does is keep my name and work in front of fans, awesome. What's the worst that can happen? They unsubscribe. If they do, awesome. They probably weren't going to buy anything in the first place. They were either being nice to me at the point of sale, or they just wanted a free book. Unsubscribes also keep my list manageable. I don't want to pay for people who aren't interested in what I'm doing.

I suppose the only negative aspect of this kind of marketing is that it does require planning and work; however, the benefits of being able to interact with fans all year long outweigh the time I spend on list maintenance, analysis, and content creation. And, like I said, it works. I've made sales, been asked to do interviews, and reconnected with past customers like Mike, a reader who bought *A Knife in the Back* at my first Awesome Con. A year after that, he read an email that I sent with my 2017 schedule, saw that I was going to Tidewater Comic-Con, stopped by my table, and bought the rest of the series (*You Will Be Safe Here* and *Burn All The Bodies*).

Start your list.

Interact with the people who like your work.

Part III Top Five Takeaways

1. Writing a book is just one part of being an indie writer. Building an audience requires marketing.

2. Marketing isn't about pushing your book on somebody. They have a need and you're trying to fulfill it.

3. Bring your work to your readers.

4. Start an email list. Offer free digital copies and send out weekly or bi-weekly newsletters about your writing life.

5. Set up automations and adjust to what your audience responds to.

Final Thoughts

My students often tell me that they truly enjoy my classes, because I "let them be who they are." I take that to mean that I'm not some kind of slave-driving Snape. After I thank them for the nice words, I add, "I hope you learned something, though."

That's my goal for whoever reads this book. That they enjoy it, find something relatable in it, and learn something useful.

Finishing any writing project is always a little bittersweet. By the time I finally feel that the work is good enough to publish, I've been over it so many times that I don't want to think about it again, at least not for a while. But that is always overridden by the excitement I feel when I start a new short story or novel. I never think "Oh man, I have to write another one," but rather "I get to do it again!" That's what drives me to write over and over, story after story, because I love doing it.

Running your own business is difficult; running your own book publishing business is even more so. There is so much self-doubt and genuine creative angst that some people choose to write in obscurity rather than work as hard as they can to let the world see what they've done. I get that. It's scary. It's a risk. And not everybody will like what you've written. Some will leave downright nasty reviews on Goodreads or opaque one stars on Amazon.

But that's how it goes.

The most important thing is to find your process, complete your work, and market it to the world. Some of the ideas will be good. Some of them won't be very good at all. That's not important. What is important is to have as much fun writing your tenth, twentieth, or thirtieth book as you did writing your first.

A NOTE FROM THE AUTHOR

Thanks again for reading *Being Indie*! One of the things that helps the most is when readers leave reviews, honest reviews, on their site of choice. If you have the time and are inclined to do so, leave one for this book!

ACKNOWLEDGMENTS

Thank you to the many authors who wrote books about indie-publishing, specifically Tim Grahl, Joanna Penn, and the Sterling and Stone crew. Without their books and information on marking and the creative mindset, I would never have felt confident enough to take the leap to authorpreneurship.

Also thank you to my Beta Readers. Without their hard work and excellent feedback, the book would have been significantly less entertaining. Angie Noll, Sandra and John Fedowitz, and Duane Pye were particularly helpful! Their notes and feedback helped me develop the third act and create a tighter, more controlled, less capricious experience.

ABOUT THE AUTHOR

James Noll is a freelance writer, an educator, a musician, and a novelist from Fredericksburg, VA. He's published several novels, a couple of short story collections, and he's produced a bunch of audiobooks. *Being Indie* is his first work of non-fiction. You can find him online at silverhammer.studio.

www.ingramcontent.com/pod-product-compliance
Lightning Source LLC
Chambersburg PA
CBHW041630220426
43665CB00001B/7